T0278034

PRAISE FOR
THE SHAPE OF JOY

"Beck reveals the toxic cultural soil in which we are all planted, which prevents us from attaining the life of meaning and fulfillment that we desire. More importantly, he offers an antidote that will allow our lives to bear the fruit of goodness and peace."

—**Falon Barton**, campus minister, University Church of Christ, Malibu, California

"For a modern world filled with anxiety and heartache, Richard Beck illuminates a path toward true and abiding happiness. The path leads us to exchange the inward focus that traps us in negativity for a life that is 'curved outward' toward love and connection. Beautifully blending psychology and spirituality, this book is a guiding light for all of us who walk in dark shadows."

—**Amy Bost-Henegar**, chaplain and pastor

"This book is a much-needed resource in our age of despair and mental anguish, a timely word addressing the current state of our mental health and the overall increase in our social decline. The path to lasting joy draws our attention beyond ourselves. The shape of joy pulls outward, beyond the self toward the sacred and holy. This book will have a life-changing impact on those who are open to its message."

—**Nathan Burrow**, preaching minister, Hillcrest Church of Christ

"In this visionary and original work, Dr. Richard Beck rises above the nonsensical self-help landscape and offers an inspiring picture of what it means to seek and obtain wonder. Beck boldly challenges our failing mental health ecosystem and the waning status quo. With the heart of a teacher, he lays out a new, research-driven path for healing our deepest individual hurts and collective cultural pain. A must-read-right-now."

—**Dr. John Delony**, *Wall Street Journal* #1 best-selling author and host of *The Dr. John Delony Show*

"Richard Beck is a master at taking complex ideas and making them accessible. *The Shape of Joy* is another example of his use of this gift. Calling it 'the geometry of self,' his use of the metaphor of geometric curves to explain the angst of our culture—particularly on the heels of the pandemic—offers a clear path forward."

—**Jackie L. Halstead,** CEO, Selah Center for Spiritual Formation, and author of *Leaning into God's Embrace: A Guidebook for Contemplative Prayer*

"Richard Beck uniquely plants himself at the complicated intersection of psychology and spirituality, sharing wisdom that seems counterintuitive to our modern sensibilities. He invites us away from the dizzying fray of our internal lives, toward one another and, ultimately, toward transcendence and the Divine. By grounding the self in a Reality beyond ourselves, we can practice and discover our way into true joy."

—**Natalie Magnusson**, assistant director for the Master of Religious Education in Missional Leadership program, Rochester Christian University

"Happiness is one thing; joy is another. Brennan Manning once lamented that some spiritual leaders are like travel agents passing out brochures promoting places that they personally have never visited. This is not that. Dr. Beck is a trustworthy guide as he leads us to look not just within but beyond ourselves."

—**Chris Seidman**, lead pastor, The Branch Church, Dallas, Texas

"Rather than inward-focused attempts at self-love and acceptance, Beck calls us to rethink the shape of joy as the embrace of quieting internal noise, rejecting the superhero complex, moving toward humility as self-forgetting, reaching out toward the needs of others, and, finally, anchoring joy in a sense of mattering through spiritual transcendence and love. Anyone interested in joy should read this book."

—**Brad D. Strawn**, Evelyn and Frank Freed Professor of the Integration of Psychology and Theology, Fuller School of Psychology & Marriage and Family Therapy; coauthor of *Enhancing Christian Life: How Extended Cognition Extends Religious Community* and coeditor of *Spiritual Diversity in Psychotherapy: Engaging the Sacred in Clinical Practice*

"*The Shape of Joy* urgently reveals not only how we lack tools to address the deprivation of joy in our lives but also how we need to dump some of the tools we assumed would help us in the first place. As a church leader, I can attest that Richard Beck has his finger on the pulse of the mental health crisis plaguing faith communities and the world. *The Shape of Joy* is for anyone looking to move past cliches and therapeutic tricks to receive the gift our hearts and minds deeply desire: joy!"

—**Zane Witcher**, lead minister, Round Rock Church of Christ, Round Rock, Texas

THE SHAPE OF JOY

RICHARD BECK

THE SHAPE OF JOY

The Transformative Power of Moving Beyond Yourself

Broadleaf Books
Minneapolis

THE SHAPE OF JOY
The Transformative Power of Moving Beyond Yourself

29 28 27 26 25 24   1 2 3 4 5 6 7 8 9

Library of Congress Control Number: 2023952464 (print)

Cover design: Brie Hattey

Print ISBN: 978-1-5064-9672-6
eBook ISBN: 978-1-5064-9807-2

Printed in China.

For Jana

CONTENTS

CONTENTS

INTRODUCTION
The Worst Graduation Speech

The year my youngest son, Aidan, graduated from high school, I was asked by his graduating class to deliver their commencement address. The talk I shared was a bit peculiar. At one point, I'm sure the audience felt they were listening to the world's worst graduation speech.

"Congratulations, graduating class of 2019!" I started on an upbeat note. So far, so good! I dutifully recognized the parents and grandparents. I thanked the faculty, staff, and administration of the school. All the normal things you say. That done, I took the talk in an unexpected direction.

"Graduates, in commencement speeches, you expect to hear something like this: 'You can be anything you want to be. Do anything you want to do. Aim high. Shoot for the stars. Follow your dreams!' But that is not what I am going to say. Because psychological research tells us that we're pretty awful at choosing what will make us happy. So here is my advice, class of 2019: do *not* follow your dreams."

I will admit I was exaggerating to make a point. But I wasn't too far from the truth. Psychological research has shown that we struggle in choosing the things that will make us happy. You've experienced this, choices large and small that didn't bring you the satisfaction or joy you had hoped for. You follow your dreams only to feel a bit let down in the end. Or arrive with a sense of regret. You climb the mountain, survey the summit, and ask, "I worked so hard, I sacrificed everything, for *this*?"

But the deeper point I wanted to make to the graduates wasn't that we struggle to make good choices. My deeper point was that even if the compass of our life were perfectly pointed toward happiness, few of us make it safely to that far shore of joy. Life gets interrupted. You took a detour, and it became the destination. Life had other plans for you. Even if your dreams point toward happiness, dreams can be broken or unfulfilled. Think back to your high school graduation, when you were told to follow your dreams. How'd that work out? Have your dreams become reality?

Life teaches you pretty quickly that dreams are fragile things.

"Few of us go from win to win in life," I said to the graduating seniors. "Maybe a lucky few of you will never face a disappointment. Never get sidetracked or lost. Perhaps you will achieve every goal you set for yourself. But the rest of us? Life isn't so easy. We get fired from jobs. We get divorced. Our phones ring with news of a diagnosis or an accident."

Looking back on this speech now, I sympathize with that poor audience. But at this dark moment, I made my final turn.

"Class of 2019, I'm not interested in the best day of your life, the day your dreams come true. That'll be an amazing day. You won't be looking around for help on the best day of your life. But we will also face some hard times and dark nights. Things won't go the way we planned. Our dreams will get broken or won't be all we had wished for."

"And so, graduates, I'm not concerned about your best day. The good days will take care of themselves. What interests me now is your worst day. Which brings me to the question I came here to ask you: *Class of 2019, how are you going to face the worst day of your life?* What will get you through your lowest point and darkest moment, when you experience heartbreak, failure, shame, and regret? Who will you be when you are holding the shattered pieces of a broken dream? How do you survive that day?"

I'm sharing my graduation speech with you to ask you the same question. What is going to happen when you arrive at your lowest point? How will you face the worst day of your life? If life is a final exam, this is the only question on the test. And everything depends on your answer.

Despite every graduation speech you've ever heard, following your dreams isn't the secret to happiness. Joy isn't ultimately found on your best day. Life is glorious when your dreams come true. The urgent, pressing question is how we face our worst days. The secret to happiness is found in the darkness.

That secret is both simple and surprising, and it boils down to psychological geometry. Joy has a shape.

Look around. The world is in pain. Mental anguish is an epidemic. Consider a new type of death we've started tracking. Never a good sign when you have to insert a new column in your spreadsheet tracking mortality statistics. Called "deaths of despair," these are deaths due to suicide, drug overdose, or liver disease from chronic alcoholism. Average life expectancies have been declining in the United States because of a sharp uptick of deaths of despair, in some demographic groups by over 300 percent. And this is just one small piece of our much larger mental health crisis. Rates of mental illness, from depression to anxiety, are rising with each new generation. And everyone, regardless of age, experiences chronic vulnerability to what some psychologists have called *derailment,* the precariousness of happiness given how our dreams and best-laid plans can be so easily knocked off course. Life is chugging along smoothly right up to the moment when the train crashes and is thrown off the railroad tracks.

Our modern vulnerabilities to both despair and derailment can be traced back to a radical change in the geometry of the self, a slow development that has happened over the last five hundred years. As the philosopher Charles Taylor has described, the self was once curved outward. Psychological stability was achieved by making contact with a transcendent, spiritual reality that existed *outside* and *beyond* the anxious drama of our inner lives. But over the last few centuries, as Taylor recounts, our mental life has slowly become curved inward upon itself. The modern ego is self-absorbed. We've become trapped within ourselves. Our struggles with both despair and derailment have emerged because of this fundamental change in the geometry of our lives. Are you *curved inward* upon yourself? Or are you *curved outward,* reaching out to connect with a transcendent, sacred reality that exists beyond yourself? On the morning of the worst day of your life, your joy will be determined by this, the shape of your soul. Geometry will determine your destiny.

The story I'll be sharing with you is about a surprising convergence between spirituality and science. Over the last few decades, psychological research investigating human happiness and flourishing has rediscovered an ancient insight taught by almost every spiritual and wisdom tradition. Transcendence is good for you. Happiness, joy, peace, meaning in life, psychological resiliency, and inner tranquilly are achieved when we pivot away from the self to find rest in a transcendent reality that exists beyond ourselves. Consider the spiritual journey of the bestselling author Brené Brown.

As she recounts in her TEDx video that launched her to superstardom, viewed now by almost sixty million people, Brown was, as a social work professor at the University of Houston, deep into her research on shame and shame resiliency. For many of us, shame is a crippling and paralyzing experience. Brown wanted to uncover the secret of those who were shame resilient. What is the secret of those who keep showing up in the face of failure, disappointment, loss, and excruciating vulnerability? Borrowing from the title of one of Brown's bestselling books, in the face of despair and derailment, what helps us keep "daring greatly" in life? As Brown recounts in her TEDx talk, she came to a shattering insight, one that precipitated a spiritual crisis in her life. That insight? There was only one characteristic that separated the shame resilient from the rest of us—the shape of joy. Brown discovered that the shame resilient possesses a single, fundamental conviction: feeling "worthy of love and belonging." This discovery triggered a personal and professional crisis for Brown because the insight is, in case you didn't notice, a bit paradoxical. Even unhelpful. For where is this conviction that I'm "worthy of love and belonging" supposed to come from? Isn't shame the experience of *not* feeling worthy of love and belonging? If so, I'm a bit stuck. You're telling me that the solution to shame is to stop feeling shame. Which is, to put it mildly, not very helpful advice.

This unhelpful contradiction at the heart of her research launched Brown on a quest, a journey where she rediscovered the wisdom of the great spiritual traditions—that our worthiness of both love and belonging comes to us as a gift. In the Christian tradition, this is called *grace*. Your value, your worthiness, is simply a truth that you embrace with gratitude. This will be your lifeline on the worst day of your life. Brown has shared how her research pointed her to this fundamental truth in the face of her own personal failures and professional disappointments:

> I put up the fight of my life, but I was totally outmatched. The universe knew exactly how to use vulnerability and uncertainty to bring down this perfectionistic shame researcher: a huge, unexpected wallop of professional failure, one devastating and public humiliation after the next, a showdown with God, strained connections with my family, anxiety so severe that I started having dizzy spells, depression, fear, and the thing that pissed me off the most—grace. No matter how hard or far I fell, grace was there to pick me up, dust me off, and shove me back in for some more.

Brené Brown's story and research are well known, and her experience illustrates what study after study has confirmed about one of the best-kept secrets of modern psychology: Faith and spirituality are consistently and reliably among the best predictors of happiness and emotional well-being. At the heart of this phenomenon is the shape of joy. Who are you on your worst day? The answer to that question isn't found by looking inward. Help comes to us from the outside, in a grace that picks you up over and over again, no matter how hard or far you fall. On your very worst day, grace tells you that you are worthy of love and belonging. Grace stands you on your feet, dusts you off, and sends you back out into the game of life.

Join me, then, as we explore the geometry of your life and the shape of your soul. Everything depends on the curvature of your life.

Our journey has three stages. In part 1, "Curved Inward," I'll recount how the modern self has experienced a catastrophic collapse. Like a cake in the oven that has failed to rise. The modern self has turned inward, becoming increasingly self-focused and self-absorbed—even self-*obsessed*—as we stew in our own anxious, ruminative juices. We are trapped in our heads. And curved inward upon ourselves, the modern mind putrefies like a stagnant pool cut off from a source of fresh water. You know what this feels like, what it's like to be too much in your own head, riding the ups and downs of your inner emotional roller coaster. In part 1, we'll survey these ailments of the modern self. I'll share stories of bike pumps, broken mirrors, and the pathology of our superhero complex.

Starting in part 2, "Turning Away," we'll begin to make a turn outward. We'll talk about the science of humility, awe, mindfulness, the small self, and ego volume. Here we'll discover that the first step toward joy is a step away from yourself. Like a blooming flower, the inwardly curved self must start to open up.

Finally, in part 3, "Curved Outward," we'll reach the heart of the book, the message I eventually shared with the class of 2019, and the truth Brené Brown discovered in her research on shame resiliency. Joy springs from the transformative power of moving beyond yourself.

Our journey will have some surprising twists and turns. So let me say something plainly if you're feeling some skepticism here at the start. Is this just another run-of-the-mill self-help and self-improvement book of the type that fills the shelves of bookstores? The answer is no. This book is different and for a simple reason. If the voice of grace is, in the end, simply your own voice, if grace is just another self-help technique, another mental mind hack, you haven't really escaped yourself. You'd still be trapped in your own head. Still curved inward. Your mind still alone, poisoning itself. This insight should be obvious, but few people pause to notice it. Spirituality is not self-help. Grace isn't grace if the voice you are hearing is simply the echo of your own. The secret to happiness isn't found in faking yourself out. To put the matter plainly, grace is only grace if grace is *real*. Grace, to be grace, is an encounter with a transcendent reality that exists independently of your own. Transcendence, going beyond yourself, isn't a therapeutic trick that keeps you talking to yourself in disguise. Grace, as a transcendent experience, isn't self-affirmation, a "You got this!" sticky note you put on the mirror. Grace *exists*, and you have to turn away from yourself to find it.

So, no, this isn't a self-help book. Self-help is exhausting. I'm inviting you to rest.

I'll leave it up to the class of 2019 to decide if what they heard was the world's worst graduation speech. For the record, I don't mind anyone following their dreams. I hope your dreams come true. But the secret of happiness will always, inevitably, come down to the darkest hour of your very worst day. That hour will be your moment of truth. And crucial to meeting that moment will be the geometry of your soul, the curvature of your mind, and the shape of your joy. On your worst day, will you be trapped within the prison of your mind, haunted by ghosts of regret and inner demons of shame? Or will you open the door to step out into the daylight of grace and the adventure of love?

At your lowest moment, I hope you choose to open the door. And if you'll let me, I'd like to show you how.

Part 1

CURVED INWARD

1 | THE COLLAPSE OF THE SELF

Times of crisis can be revelations. Sometimes in the middle of the storm, we find that we can stand. We discover a strength we didn't know we possessed. But crises can also expose weaknesses, the fractures in the foundation of our society, our relationships, and our mental stability. The wind blows, and life comes crashing down.

The COVID-19 pandemic revealed some things about us. Some beautiful things emerged during our lockdowns. Like many, I learned to bake bread. We cherished slower rhythms and used the space to rethink and recalibrate. While we wanted life to get back to "normal" as quickly as possible, we didn't want life to resume exactly as it had before. We wanted to enter the post-COVID world as better people who lived slower, richer, and more intentional lives. We wanted to invest more deeply in relationships we had been neglecting.

COVID-19 also revealed some pathologies, sicknesses in our society and in ourselves. A slowly metastasizing cancer finally came into view. The symptoms of this disease were various, but two major ones caught our collective attention.

Do you remember our debates about the effectiveness of masks? Or about the safety of vaccines? Do you remember the wild cures being proposed, from injecting bleach to taking medicine used for deworming horses? While hospitals overflowed and the death toll climbed, some even denied that the virus was real.

Before COVID-19, we knew our shared vision of reality was splintering. It wasn't just that we were politically polarized and had strong ideological disagreements. The problem went deeper. We knew we were living in echo chambers, but COVID-19 revealed that we had come to inhabit alternative realities. We discovered we existed in different worlds. Truth itself was up for grabs. Your facts were my fake news.

Our rage and despair skyrocketed. Our neighbors, coworkers, and family members seemed literally insane, in the grip of paranoid delusions. We couldn't talk to each other because we had no common reference point, no shared vision of reality. People were dying, and hospitals overflowed. Our generational moment of truth had arrived. The bell of history was calling us to heroic action. But we couldn't agree on anything. Reality had become a Rorschach inkblot. Facts were open to interpretation. We projected onto the world our paranoia and fear, and each of us saw a very different boogeyman. And far too often, we saw each other as the monster.

If the first thing COVID-19 exposed was this fracturing of truth, the second thing that came into view was our increasingly fragile mental health. We were already struggling before COVID-19, but the pandemic pushed us over the edge. During COVID-19, rates of depression, anxiety, substance use, overdose deaths, and suicide all increased. Collectively, we just cracked. The Centers for Disease Control and Prevention reported that, during the pandemic, 41 percent of Americans were dealing with a significant mental health issue. And even if we didn't suffer from acute mental illness, the lockdowns revealed a vacuum in our lives, an existential hole. Unable to go out to eat, attend a movie, or hit the clubs, we found the hollowness of our lives exposed. A life full of distractions and entertainments had kept us from taking a hard look in the mirror. The lockdowns left us alone with ourselves, and we found that experience sad and unsettling. Not surprisingly, we found an easy way to avoid facing ourselves: we drank more alcohol. COVID-19 didn't kill us, but many of us drank ourselves to death.

On the surface, it might not seem like debates about masks and increased suicide risk have a lot to do with each other. But these are symptoms of the same disease, the runny nose and the high fever caused by the same underlying illness. The loss of our shared vision of reality and our mental health crisis are each rooted in a profound change that has affected the geometry of the self. COVID-19 revealed how the modern mind had collapsed upon itself, trapping and imprisoning us within ourselves. The consequences of this collapse were there for everyone to see: our mental health has been radically destabilized, and the very nature of reality is now up for grabs.

If you want to know how all this happened, pull up a chair. Let me tell you the story.

A man sits in a room and doubts that the world exists.

That chair across the room? Could be a figment of my imagination. My warm cup of coffee? I could be dreaming. Maybe, like Keanu Reeves, we're plugged into the Matrix! The world is just a virtual reality simulation. Maybe we're a brain in a vat, a favorite thought experiment of philosophers, where some advanced alien species has wired up our brains and is sending us false sensory inputs. Maybe nothing is real!

This sort of radical skepticism—reality is a hallucination, a simulation, a dream!—seems to be the stuff of science fiction and sophomore dorm-room debates. But there was a man who once sat in a room and doubted that the world existed. His meditations about this skepticism changed the course of the modern world and contributed to the slow collapse of the self.

Our skeptic was René Descartes (1596–1650), the famous French mathematician and philosopher. Your first exposure to Descartes was likely in middle school when you encountered the x- and y-axes of the Cartesian coordinate system. Remember $y = mx + b$? Descartes invented that stuff. Beyond creating analytic geometry, the fusion of algebra and geometry, Descartes was also a philosopher, and his most influential and significant book was entitled *Meditations on First Philosophy*, often just called *Meditations*.

The puzzle Descartes set before himself in *Meditations* seems obscure, but it has had far-reaching implications. Descartes wanted to establish the certainty of knowledge, a foolproof way of establishing the truth. You could, for example, really be dreaming right now. I might be dreaming I'm writing this sentence on my laptop. This is unlikely, but it is possible. If so, how could you ever establish—for a fact and beyond a shadow of a doubt—that the book you are holding in your hands right now is real?

Seeking a way to answer this question, Descartes goes big. He clears the floor. He begins by doubting the reality of everything he sees, hears, smells, and feels. Descartes assumes the world is a figment of his imagination. He then attempts to build up from scratch, bit by bit, establishing truth and reality every step of the way.

This exercise in what has been called *Cartesian doubt* radically altered the shape of the self. In doubting the existence of the world, Descartes withdraws within himself. Reality becomes compressed to a single point, a psychic singularity, a psychological black hole. With the whole of reality radically rejected, Descartes is left only with himself, the lonely boat of his ego afloat on a dark sea of doubt. All that exists, with 100 percent certainty, is me.

That's Descartes's starting point. We *know* we *exist* because we can *think* about ourselves. The reality of my own existence is the very first thing I can prove. As Descartes famously intoned, "Cogito, ergo sum." I think, therefore I am.

Descartes's insight here seems obvious and trivial. If you're thinking about yourself, you have to exist. This is a pretty foolproof argument. Clear and logical. But with Descartes's "I think, therefore I am," a fateful threshold was crossed in human history. A corner was turned. And the world would never be the same.

With Descartes, the geometry of our experience of the world was flipped inside out. Prior to Descartes, truth was established by making *contact* with a *reality* that existed *outside* my head and *beyond* myself. And for most of human history, the most important part of this reality was a sacred transcendence, an encounter with God. The Reality behind our reality. Descartes flipped this script by *doubting the whole of reality* in an exercise of *radical skepticism*. All of reality is called into question. For Descartes, truth doesn't start with *reality*, coming to know and agree with something that exists independently of myself. Truth collapses upon the isolated ego. Truth starts with *me*. I become the arbiter and judge of what is or is not real. The only thing you can be certain of is yourself.

This wasn't what Descartes intended. He had hoped that his exercise in radical skepticism would further the role of reason, logic, and rationality in the establishment of truth. And the *Meditations* was an influential book in kicking off the Enlightenment and launching the Age of Reason. Descartes's use of doubt and skepticism was embraced as wrecking balls that could destroy ancient dogma, religious superstition, pious tradition, social taboos, and church authority. Doubt became the acid of the Enlightenment, used to dissolve the dusty certainties of the ancient world and launching us into a freethinking future of technological progress and social liberation. But radical doubt opened Pandora's box. If you doubt the existence of everything, then everything can be doubted. Descartes tried to draw some lines in the sand, places where the acid of doubt could not reach. But very quickly, those lines were crossed, and widespread skepticism came to characterize the modern world. Eventually, we reached the predictable outcome that COVID-19 exposed: Reality now *itself* is questioned. Facts are doubted. Science is fake news.

When Descartes withdrew from the world into himself, the isolated ego gained the power to question and doubt anything in reality. Suddenly, everything about our crisis of truth during the pandemic snaps into clear focus. No purported "fact" now stands a chance as the self can doubt anything it pleases. When the self collapsed, truth evaporated. Starting with Descartes, we've been set free to construct a world of our own choosing, sculpting the "facts" to support any vision of reality we find compelling. You'll have your truth, and I'll have mine.

Beyond creating our post-truth world, the collapse of the self also undermined our mental health and emotional resiliency. When the ego turned away from reality to make itself the ultimate arbiter of truth, it also turned away from sacred narratives, symbols, values, and rituals that once provided us with meaning, significance, and purpose in life. Throughout human history, psychological stability was achieved by connecting with a sacred and spiritual reality that existed independently of our own neuroses. We found rest in this reality because it didn't depend on us. Sacred truths, transcendent values, and spiritual realities didn't have to be made up or invented. Nor were they affected by the ups and downs of life. Where our days are variable and changeable, swinging from highs to lows, the spiritual world was constant and unchanging. The ego could stand amid the storms of life because it clung to a sacred stability infinitely more solid than itself.

To be sure, our experience of transcendence goes by many names. The Greeks called it the True, the Beautiful, and the Good. People sitting in the chairs of an Alcoholics Anonymous meeting call it their Higher Power. Indigenous Americans pray to the Great Spirit. Most people call it God. The Christian mystic Pseudo-Dionysius, who wrote in the sixth century, described this transcendent reality as "the cause of everything" and as the "sacred stability" that grounds and supports our lives. As Pseudo-Dionysius describes, we use a host of words to capture our encounter with transcendence: *Being, Source, Creator, Love, Goodness, Center, Unity, Spirit, Savior, Grace*, and *Light*. But ultimately, declares Pseudo-Dionysius, this reality is, in the final analysis, "the Nameless One," transcending all human categorization, verbal description, and rational comprehension.

However conceived or culturally described, our lives were once held, valued, and directed by this Beauty, Love, and Light. The geometry of our lives was directed *outward* toward our Source. Psychologically, this sacred grounding provided us with a firm, stable platform on which to stand. It still does. As I've said, one of the most consistent findings but carefully held secrets in the field of psychology is how faith and spirituality support psychological health. But on reflection, this relationship shouldn't be all that surprising. When life comes crashing down and we stand, ashamed and lost, in the rubble of failure and regret, we find shelter where the value and meaning of our lives are held safe, secure, and inviolate. The ancient Hebrews turned toward this Comfort when they prayed:

> God is our refuge and strength,
> a very present help in trouble.
> Therefore we will not fear, though the earth should
>   change,
> though the mountains shake in the heart of the sea,
> though its waters roar and foam,
> though the mountains tremble with its tumult. (Ps
>   46:1–3)

Held by a transcendent Source of comfort, we find a safe haven, a protected harbor when the storms of life howl with hurricane force. Without this Refuge, the ego is left alone and naked, exposed to the icy blasts of rejection, loss, self-defeating behaviors, broken dreams, failure, and catastrophe. When we stand isolated and bereft of help, we take it all directly in the face. All the pain, despair, stress, fear, and trauma. We shiver in the cold, battered and bruised, with no hope of support or rescue.

The greatest tragedy of modern life is that we have willfully turned our back on this comfort. We've closed in on ourselves and looked away from the Sacred Source of our being. We've jettisoned the lifeboats. Cut the powerlines. Hung up the phone. The mental health consequences of this fateful turn have been disastrous. The ego needs a protected, safe place to rest and rehabilitate. A place where wounds are healed, fears soothed, and courage regained. Lacking this, the ego grows weary, and the damage of life, often self-inflicted, accumulates like scar tissue. Eventually, cracks appear. Chronic stress. Crippling shame. Debilitating depression. Free-floating anxiety. Growing addiction.

If René Descartes started the collapse of the self, Sigmund Freud brought it to its fateful conclusion. Sigmund Freud (1856–1939) was the key player in what we might call the *therapeutic turn* in the modern world. Pioneer of psychoanalysis—the "talking cure," where somatic and psychological symptoms could be resolved through verbally processing their traumatic origins—and spelunker of the dark caverns of the unconscious, Freud has left a deep and lasting imprint on our collective imagination. Almost every cultural assumption we have regarding mental health and dysfunction goes back to him. We joke that "denial" isn't just a river in Egypt. We tell a coworker to stop being so "defensive." We comment that a friend has "daddy issues" or is a "momma's boy." We insist that we must "talk through" our feelings, that we shouldn't "bottle up" our anger, and that we need to "blow off some steam." We describe traditional sexual codes of conduct as "repressive." Our emotions often feel "conflicted." Obsessive-compulsive tendencies are described as "anal," short for "anal retentive." We become "fixated" on things. We "analyze" our dreams, looking for hidden meanings. We try to "compensate" for our insecurities. We have "slips" of the tongue.

Sigmund Freud is the air we breathe. We're all Freudian.

Critical to the therapeutic turn led by Freud was *an inward turn*, just like René Descartes. But where Descartes turned inward for *truth*, Freud turned inward for *health*. For Freud, emotional stability was achieved not by reaching upward and outward toward sources of transcendent comfort and support but by plumbing the murky depths of the unconscious psyche. Mental health is found by doing a deep dive into yourself to confront and sort through the traumas of your past. To heal, you need to go inside to discover the hidden sources of your hurt, knitting that pain, in a meaningful way, into the story of your life. This healing process is akin to Japanese kintsugi art, where gold is used to mend cracked pottery. We can't avoid the broken parts of life, but we are called to transform them into something beautiful. As Leonard Cohen sings, "There is a crack in everything, that's how the light gets in."

In theory, that's how psychological healing is supposed to work. And it often does. But as Freud went on to elucidate, achieving wholeness is complicated by our expertise in obfuscation and avoidance. It's almost impossible to get a clear, honest view of yourself. The cracks aren't exactly where we think they are. You never really know if you're telling yourself the truth. Plus, progress can be elusive and fleeting. The "breakthrough" I experienced this week in therapy can be as short-lived as a New

Year's resolution. Psychologically, you're always taking one step forward and two steps back.

The reason for this, Freud said, is because we are enigmas to ourselves, full of contradiction and paradox. We are masters of self-deception. Living "my truth" is often just living a lie.

How, then, are we ever going to escape the maze of ourselves and crawl out of the caverns of our unconscious mind?

Well, opined Dr. Freud, what you need is a seasoned, experienced guide. You need an expert in psychoanalysis! That was the snake oil Freud was selling. Sadly, though, the promise of psychoanalysis was very short-lived. Classic psychoanalysis, as practiced by Freud, is pretty much extinct. Freud couldn't deliver what he promised the modern world. As the old joke goes, sometimes a cigar is just a cigar.

What happened to Descartes happened to Freud. Descartes turned inward, toward the self, hoping to secure the truth. Instead, the truth was destroyed. The self was liberated to doubt anything it wanted. Any fact can now be called "fake news." In a similar way, Freud turned inward, promising to secure our mental health in the trusted pronouncements of the psychoanalyst. But when psychoanalysis was revealed to be hokum, we were abandoned by our guide to wander the corridors of the mind alone and unaided. Freud led us deep into the caves of the mind, promising he had a map and a flashlight to guide us back out. But once we got lost in the darkness, we discovered he had neither.

The story I've shared here is selective and simplified. But there's broad agreement among scholars that both Descartes and Freud, for the reasons we've just discussed, were critical players in the collapse of the self. The modern ego is a novelty, an innovation. New to history. Trying to capture this change, the Canadian philosopher Charles Taylor describes the modern self as "buffered." According to Taylor, our prior, ancient self was experienced as "porous." In the experience of the porous self, the boundary between the ego and the external world was permeable. Forces in the external world could affect me, could impinge on and even invade my self. The porous self could be hexed and cursed, possessed by devils or open to the guidance of God. The modern self, by contrast, is experienced as closed and walled off from the world, especially from supernatural influences and spiritual realities. This buffered self stands isolated and alone, cut off from the world.

While I understand the point Taylor is making in grabbing the word *buffered* to describe the modern self, I think a deeper and more accurate picture is gained if we appropriate a description of the self that goes back to St. Augustine. In Latin, the modern self is *incurvatus in se* (curved inward), upon itself. The modern self isn't just buffered; it is *curved*. What Descartes and Freud did was to fundamentally alter the *geometry* of the self. As we've seen, the ancient self was curved *outward*—we were once *excurvatus ex se*. This outwardly curved self was oriented away from itself toward external reality, especially transcendent truths and values. When I describe joy having a shape, this curvature is what I am describing. Are we curved *inward* or *outward*? *Incurvatus in se* or *excurvatus ex se*? The question is vital and pressing because an inwardly curved self—being *incurvatus in se*—has disrupted and destabilized the modern world. Both truth and joy have gone missing. And it's all due to psychological geometry.

As much as I'd love to dig deeper into the crisis of truth in our world—from fake news to science denialism—we're going to keep our focus on joy going forward. I want to show you how being *incurvatus in se,* being curved inward upon yourself, wrecks your mental health.

Our psychological fragility demands a closer, more surgical look.

2 | BIKE PUMPS AND CIGARETTES

Getting into my car, I noticed a slow leak in one of the tires. The tire had lost enough air that I didn't want to drive it to a gas station. But the tire wasn't so completely flat that I needed to jack up the car and bust out the spare. I stood there between options, wishing I had one of those electronic air pumps that I could plug in and inflate my tire right there in the driveway. Pondering that machine, I realized I didn't need an electronic gadget. I had something at the house that could inflate the tire manually. The valve on my bike pump would fit the valve on my car tire.

I retrieved the bike pump from the shed and fitted it to the tire valve. I began to pump. It worked like a charm, but I quickly made a discovery: it is exhausting to inflate a car tire with a bike pump.

My neighbors, I expect, thought I'd lost my mind, watching me furiously pumping away, trying to fill my flat tire. I didn't mind looking crazy, but I quickly wore myself out.

The modern self is just like inflating a car tire with a bike pump. It is an exhausting project. Every day, we awake to the task of becoming the self we aspire to or the self we want others to like or admire. We try, in the language of Maslow's hierarchy of needs, to "self-actualize." We "perform" the self, like an actor taking the stage before an audience. You perform for your boss, your family, your friends. A lot of your performance probably takes place on social media, as you carefully crop and curate your image and self-presentation. Sustaining this performance demands constant energy and effort, like trying to keep a leaky car tire inflated with a bike pump. Eventually, this exertion takes a toll, and you burn out.

The frantic effort we put into performing the self is a modern affliction. After the self collapsed, it has demanded constant reinflation. Being a self has become effortful, energy-consuming work, birthing uniquely modern pathologies and dysfunctions. Here's how Matthew Crawford has described our challenges in performing and actualizing the modern self:

> Once upon a time, our problem was guilt: the feeling that you have made a mistake, with reference to something forbidden. This was felt as a stain on one's character. . . . [Today] the dichotomy of the forbidden and the allowed has been replaced with an axis of the possible and the impossible. The question that hovers over your character is no longer that of how good you are, but of how capable you are, where capacity is measured in something like Kilowatt hours—the raw capacity to make things happen. With this shift comes a new pathology. The affliction of guilt has given way to weariness—weariness with the vague and unending project of having to become one's fullest self. We call this depression.

In describing this "weariness of the self," Alain Ehrenberg observes, "Depression presents itself as an illness of responsibility in which the dominant feeling is that of failure. The depressed individual is unable to measure up; he is tired of having to become himself."

Brené Brown describes the weariness we experience in not being able to measure up as "the never enough problem," a felt experience of scarcity. As Brown describes, "Scarcity is the 'never enough' problem. . . . Scarcity thrives in a culture where everyone is hyperaware of lack. Everything from safety and love to money and resources feels restricted or lacking. We spend inordinate amounts of time calculating how much we have, want, and don't have, and how much everyone else has, needs, and wants."

Scarcity is what we experience when the self collapses. We feel depleted, empty, drained, and lacking, like a flat tire in the driveway. Lynne Twist walks us through the daily exhaustion we feel facing the "vague and unending project of having to become one's fullest self":

For me, and for many of us, our first waking thought of the day is "I didn't get enough sleep." The next one is "I don't have enough time." Whether true or not, that thought of not enough occurs to us automatically before we even think to question or examine it. We spend most of the hours and the days of our lives hearing, explaining, complaining, or worrying about what we don't have enough of. . . . Before we even sit up in bed, before our feet touch the floor, we're already inadequate, already behind, already losing, already lacking something. And by the time we go to bed at night, our minds are racing with a litany of what we didn't get, or didn't get done, that day. We go to sleep burdened by those thoughts and wake up to that reverie of lack. . . . This internal condition of scarcity, this mind-set of scarcity, lives at the very heart of our jealousies, our greed, our prejudice, and our arguments with life.

The modern self wakes up each morning to a "reverie of lack," obsessing and ruminating over our particular and private never-enough problems. We start the day already behind, already losing. The modern self just isn't "enough" all on its own. And so, we feverishly work and perform to fill it up, to reinflate the flat tire. But the effort is exhausting and simply creates a new set of scarcities—no energy, no time, no mental space, no margin, no rest. We are caught in what I call a scarcity trap, where dealing with scarcities in one area of life creates scarcities elsewhere. Dealing with a scarcity at work—like getting caught up—creates a scarcity at home. Dealing with a scarcity of sleep by sleeping in causes us to miss going to the gym, creating a scarcity of exercise. You go on vacation but return to a mountain of work. Scarcity is a whack-a-mole problem. We can't keep up. Filling in one hole just creates a hole elsewhere. Swimming furiously, you realize that you are slowly drowning.

Sometimes what you think is good for you might actually be killing you. A notorious example happened during the 1930s and '40s when doctors recommended cigarette smoking to reduce throat irritation. That medical advice didn't age very well. We're facing a similar problem when it comes to our current mental health crisis. We are mistaking a poison for a cure.

Our never-enough problems are problems of our own making. We are working with a widespread assumption about how to achieve mental health and psychological resiliency that is deeply mistaken. This assumption shows up everywhere, a belief that guides our parenting, educational systems, and therapeutic enterprises. The idea is this: we think that happiness involves the enhancement of *self-esteem*. We are attempting joy through self-regard. This is the bike pump we are working at so feverishly, our collective attempt to solve the never-enough problem through the "vague and unending project of having to become one's fullest self." If we want to be happy, we think, we need to possess a good opinion of ourselves, especially in how we compare with others. And if we don't hold this good opinion, the logic continues, then our inevitable personal insecurities and social anxieties will cripple our mental health. The therapeutic imperative here is crystal clear: *you* need to feel *better* about *yourself*.

And that's the precise moment we step into the quicksand.

Self-esteem is a trap. We're smoking cigarettes mistaking them for medicine.

Now, it is true that low self-esteem is associated with psychological dysfunction. Studies have shown this. So it's not unreasonable to think that rehabilitating self-esteem would be helpful. But self-esteem is, at best, a temporary fix. Self-esteem works right up until the moment you bump into your next failure. This makes self-esteem a never-ending and exhausting project: we have to keep rehabilitating our self-assessments, over and over again. This constant reinflation of our deflated self-image is what produces weariness with the self. It is high time we stop pumping up the flat car tire to focus on patching the leak.

To see how self-esteem wearies the self, let's go back to the very first appearance self-esteem made in the field of psychology. In 1890, the famous psychologist and philosopher William James published one of the very first psychology textbooks. Entitled *Principles of Psychology*, James's textbook has had an enormous impact, to this very day. For example, it's in *Principles of Psychology* where James famously describes our waking experience as the "stream of consciousness." And it's also in *Principles of Psychology* where William James presented the first psychological definition and description of self-esteem.

According to him, our self-esteem, our "average tone of self-feeling," is the outcome of a psychological calculation, specifically a division. And James shares the formula. He writes that self-esteem "is determined by the ratio of our actualities to our supposed potentialities; a fraction of which our pretensions are the denominator and the numerator our success: thus, Self-esteem = Success / Pretensions."

Basically, self-esteem is the ratio of our successes divided by our pretensions. By "pretensions," James means our goals, the life we desire and want. Self-esteem, then, is an emotional feeling that measures the degree to which the life we have—what we have been "successful" in securing for ourselves—matches the life we want. Even more simply, self-esteem measures the *gap* between the actual and the ideal. For example, if you've been successful in achieving "your best life now," your self-esteem will be high. You'll be feeling good about yourself because the life you have matches the life you want. Conversely, if you've been unsuccessful in realizing "your best life now," your self-esteem will be low. You'll be feeling bad about yourself because you've failed to achieve your dreams.

You don't need to be a rocket scientist to see how foolish it has been to base our mental health on this calculation. We're smoking psychological cigarettes here, and you can see the problem right there in the very first psychological definition of self-esteem. Stated bluntly, self-esteem is *an emotional metric of dissatisfaction.* James's definition of self-esteem reminds me of the London subway system, where a recorded voice reminds you to "mind the gap" as you step from train to platform. That's what self-esteem does—it minds the gap. Self-esteem monitors the distance between the life you *have* and the life you *want*, what you *wish for* and what you *get*, what you *dream of* and what you *settle for*. Self-esteem measures the size of your dissatisfaction.

You can see the disaster brewing. We are building our mental health on an emotional metric that keeps track of our failure. No wonder our mental health is in freefall.

The problem here isn't just with the emotional *content* of self-esteem, the gap between our dreams and disappointments. The problem is also that esteem is a *measurement*, an emotional feedback system. Since life is full of successes and failures, self-esteem goes up and down, reflecting those changes. As a feedback system, self-esteem is like the stock market. Sometimes the market goes up, and sometimes it crashes. Self-esteem is an inner emotional ticker tape keeping track of how well your life is going at this moment. And depending on the day, sometimes we're up, and sometimes we're down.

The trap isn't just that self-esteem tracks the disaffections of my life, always minding the gap between my successes and failures; it's also that self-esteem is, by its very nature, *variable*—it goes up and down. Again, you can see the obvious problem. In the storms of life, we need psychological *stability*, a firm place to stand. We want deep roots to hold us in place. What we don't need is something that *goes up and down*. When the hurricane blows, self-esteem isn't a storm cellar; it's a weather vane.

But psychological science has made a lot of progress since 1890, when William James first introduced self-esteem to the world. Perhaps we have better understandings of self-esteem today, making our decision to view it as the key to mental health less of a train wreck. Sadly, things haven't gotten any better.

Consider the modern and very influential "sociometer" theory of self-esteem by psychologists Mark Leary and Roy Baumeister. According to Leary and Baumeister, self-esteem has less to do with successes and failures, as William James believed, and more to do with our social relationships. Self-esteem, in this view, is an internal emotional thermometer telling us how socially valued and loved we are. The temperature of this social thermometer—a sociometer—can be high (you feel welcomed, loved, and included) or low (you feel rejected, alone, and unloved). Here's Leary and Baumeister describing the idea: "According to sociometer theory, self-esteem serves as a subjective monitor of one's relational evaluation—the degree to which other people regard their relationships with the individual to be valuable, important, or close. Put somewhat differently, the self-esteem system monitors one's eligibility for lasting, desirable relationships, including membership in important small groups. The self-esteem system is essentially a sociometer that monitors the quality of an individual's interpersonal relationships and motivates behaviors that help the person to maintain a minimum level of acceptance by other people."

As a bit of innate relational software, having a sociometer in your head makes perfect adaptive sense. Humans are profoundly social creatures, so we need something in our brains telling us how well our relationships are going. If we're alienating people, we need some emotional feedback to help us adapt and change in social contexts. If people don't like me, I need to know that if I want to build healthy relationships. There's a reason why we experience loneliness as painful. That pain nudges us to seek connection, like hunger nudges us toward food. The sociometer also rewards us with warm, fuzzy feelings when we experience intimacy and love. These positive vibes reward interpersonal behaviors that facilitate our connections with others.

All this makes perfect sense. We *need* a sociometer. We'd be lost socially without it. But a sociometer is a *disastrous* thing to depend on for mental health, for the exact same reasons we observed with William James's view of self-esteem. Once again, a sociometer is a *meter*, a measuring device, an emotional feedback loop. And being a meter, the sociometer is *supposed to* go up and down as we experience either rejection or love. That's its purpose, to register how things are going for us, good or bad, in the world of intimacy and affection. Consequently, it is crazy to build mental health on something so variable, changing, and inconstant.

And the problem with the sociometer goes even deeper. As I've pointed out, we need something to lean on when we experience rejection, loss, and heartbreak. And it's precisely in those moments when the sociometer is going to fail you. In fact, when you're at your lowest moment, the sociometer will just show up to kick you in the teeth. Seriously, what is the sociometer telling you when you get divorced? Or go through a period of loneliness? What does the sociometer have to say when you get stabbed in the back by a friend? Or can't find a date or anyone to fall in love with? We know *exactly* what the sociometer will shout at you: "You are worthless! No one likes you! No one wants you!" Self-esteem—in either the sociometer or mind-the-gap varieties—is *not* what we need in these moments. In fact, *self-esteem is the problem here*, that voice in your head informing you of your failure or that you are unlovable. What we need in moments of loss and grief is something that helps us escape this trap, something that turns us away from that negative inner voice and gets us out of our heads.

When we look at William James's formula for self-esteem—self-esteem = successes / pretentions—there does seem to be a way to escape the trap of dissatisfaction. If I'm struggling with being successful, could I not just lower my expectations? Couldn't I work the pretention side of the equation and reduce the denominator?

There is a truth here. Disappointment has a lot to do with expectations. In my own life, as a self-protective measure, I regularly keep my expectations low to avoid disappointment. I try to set my pretentions to zero. I'd rather be pleasantly surprised than bitterly disappointed. Consequently, I often find myself expecting the worst. But rehearsing disasters in your head isn't the best recipe for happiness.

The more difficult and deeper problem here is how our expectations are products of social comparison. We want to compare well with others, and everyone seems to be climbing. So we rush to keep up. And if we start slowing down while everyone keeps moving closer to their dreams, we worry that we are settling. We grow anxious because we're being left behind as friends and family keep reaching that next milestone. Social media has made this sort of social comparison a daily emotional confrontation, a virtual mirror that reflects our failure and mediocrity. Our lives feel chronically diminished by the successes of others. We steep in envy and insecurity. And keeping up becomes an exhausting project.

Author Alain de Botton has described the stress we experience in social comparison as "status anxiety," which he defines as "a worry, so pernicious as to be capable of ruining extended stretches of our lives, that we are in danger of failing to conform to the ideals of success laid down by our society and that we may as a result be stripped of dignity and respect; a worry that we are currently occupying too modest a rung or are about to fall to a lower one." This pervasive status anxiety is what makes it so difficult to lower our expectations in the equation of self-esteem. When we fail to meet cultural standards of success, we fear the loss of respect, value, worth, and dignity. Shame keeps us pushing.

As described by de Botton, status anxiety is a modern ailment, associated with capitalism and its meritocracy. In pre-industrial cultures, the wealth of individuals was regulated by agriculture. In that world, landowners were rich, and workers were poor. Further, given that land was handed down through families, it was impossible for a poor laborer to change their situation. The land—the main route to wealth—was all owned. Consequently, the social and economic classes were stratified in agrarian, preindustrial societies. To say nothing about slavery. More than stratified, social class was petrified. Little movement occurred. If you were born a peasant or a slave, you died a peasant or a slave. And you couldn't be judged or blamed for this outcome. It was just your lot in life.

But with the advent of the technological revolution and modern economies, all this has changed. In our world, wealth is no longer solely tied to land. With technological innovation came entrepreneurship, effort, and ingenuity. If you had grit, determination, and a strong work ethic, a person born into poverty could escape the slums and trailer parks. For the first time in history, a person could climb the social ladder. And they did. The old aristocratic class system was slowly dismantled. New money began to mix with the old.

But the advent of the American dream—everyone can make it—came with a price. For better or worse, we've become *responsible* for our *success* in life. The peasant or slave of bygone eras had to settle for their lot in life. They had no other choice. But in our world, to settle is to be a slacker. The cream rises to the top. You must climb. To be *poor* is to be *blameworthy*. In the modern world, failure is a mark of character. Mediocrity is our new scarlet letter.

Our meritocratic society, where people are believed to get what they deserve, is infused with status anxiety. If you fail, you're damaged goods. Too dumb, lazy, or weak. You deserve your place in life. As de Botton describes, our dignity/value now "hangs on what we can achieve . . . and from failure will flow humiliation: A corroding awareness that we have been unable to convince the world of our value and are henceforth condemned to consider the successful with bitterness and ourselves with shame."

Status anxiety is why we find modern life so exhausting. The rat race isn't just about putting food on the table. We're competing for dignity. Your *value* as a human being is now something you can *lose*. It's just one failure away. This makes it impossible to step off the hamster wheel. Your resume is your worth. We have to succeed so that people will see us. Otherwise, we're just some loser standing alone in a corner. We've got to work some angle, some way to shine and stand out. We are whip-poor-wills of insecurity chirping out, "Look at me, look at me, look at me!"

When you step back to consider the nature of self-esteem, it's obvious that no one should ever have trusted it as a reliable foundation for joy. As an emotional feedback system, self-esteem just reports about how well your life is going. And when life isn't going very well, self-esteem is the very thing we find ourselves combating. When the voice in our head breaks the news that "you have just failed" or "you have just been rejected," where are we to turn for support and comfort?

It could be argued that self-esteem doesn't have to be an emotional *feedback* system. Self-esteem could just be a self-*evaluation*, a positive and unconditional acceptance of the self. As Brené Brown has argued, shame resiliency flows out of seeing yourself as "worthy of love and belonging." Achieving this steady and positive view of yourself—learning to love and accept yourself—is what most of us are trying to do to improve self-esteem. But I'm sad to share that this view of *self-esteem as self-affirmation* also has its problems.

The first problem is that you're trying to turn self-esteem into something it isn't. We're exhausting ourselves talking back to a voice in our heads because that voice never stops; it never shuts up. Despite your best efforts, the voice of self-esteem, as an emotional feedback system, will maintain its steady flow of news flashes: "You have just failed!" and "You have just been rejected!" And in the face of those hourly reports, we have to keep expending energy to beat back the darkness. Day in and day out, we spend enormous amounts of energy talking back to ourselves. Self-affirmation is wearying. Especially when we have actually failed and been rejected, when the ugly facts are staring us in the face. We need comfort in these moments, not another inner debate with ourselves.

But the more tragic problem here isn't the exhaustion of perpetually talking back to your inner emotional newsflashes about yet another "terrible, horrible, no good, very bad day." Sometimes a self-image can be so damaged that it just can't be rehabilitated.

With my students, I call it the "broken mirror" problem of self-esteem. We think of self-esteem as a mirror, a reflection of how we see ourselves. And wanting to embrace self-love and affirmation, we look into that mirror and say things like Al Franken's *SNL* Stuart Smalley character: "I'm good enough, I'm smart enough, and doggone it, people like me!" But sometimes, beyond the exhaustion of this daily effort, the mirror itself gets cracked. And when the mirror cracks, we might never be able to see ourselves in a healthy or positive way again. The obvious examples here are trauma and abuse. Things happen to us through no fault of our own that permanently damage our self-perceptions. To be clear, I'm not saying damage is destiny, that victims can't live full and happy lives. Just that the bad things that happen to us can haunt us, often for our entire lives. Whenever we look at ourselves, there's a crack in the mirror that never quite goes away. And no amount of therapy or medication seems to remove it.

The tragic thing is that most of these cracks don't come from trauma or abuse. The cracks originate from the sad but predictable hurts of everyday life. When you ask people about the origins of their negative self-image, where the crack in their mirror came from, they will tell you stories. Something happened or was said to them that became internalized, like a thorn in the mind, as "the truth" about themselves. A comment from a parent, teacher, or coach about their body, talent, or worth. A joke in a locker room or school hallway that shamed you. Being teased in middle school. Something said in the heat of a fight with a lover or spouse. At the heart of our insecurities, there's always an origin story, something that cut or shamed us. Maybe it was a long and prolonged season of pain or abuse, or maybe it was quick and fast like the stab of a knife. But whatever it was, it cracked the mirror, and we've never had a clear view of ourselves since.

I have been a therapist, father, husband, sibling, friend, coach, teacher, mentor, and pastor. And I can tell you this, something you already know: you can't talk people out of these cracks. I've tried to talk people out of these cracks, and so have you. But self-esteem can't be talked into people. Words don't repair the mirror, not fully or completely. Nor can a drug prescription, as helpful and lifesaving as those can be.

I deeply sympathize with how hard we all work at self-love, care, and affirmation. We're all cracked mirrors. But I bet you're exhausting yourself trying to patch yourself up, along with everyone else in your life. Something has gone very wrong in our efforts to help each other and ourselves because all this work doesn't seem to be helping very much. We're pumping away at those bike pumps, but the air keeps escaping.

The trap we're all caught in is that we've become fixated on how we think and feel about ourselves. We're stuck inside ourselves, our mental wheels spinning in the mud of failure and rejection. Our self-ruminations are imprisoning us. We obsessively keep looking at ourselves in the mirror, over and over again. But that is the very source of our problem, how our self-conceptions have become so self-referential, like a dog chasing its tail. We expect this thing that is broken—myself—to be a tool that will fix me. Our self-recriminations perpetually debate our self-affirmations like a deadlocked jury that can't reach a verdict.

This is the trap of self-esteem.

We've been smoking cigarettes our entire lives mistaking them for a cure.

3 | THE SUPERHERO COMPLEX

On December 4, 2016, at around 3:00 p.m., Edgar Welch entered the restaurant with his AR-15 assault rifle and began firing. But what unfolded that day wasn't another mass shooting tragedy. Welch didn't hurt anyone. Welch had come to the Washington, DC, pizza joint Comet Ping Pong because he wanted to be a hero. As Welch later recounted in court documents, "I just wanted to do some good."

Edgar Welch drove to Comet Ping Pong with heroic intentions because he had been taken in by the conspiracy theory known as PizzaGate. According to the PizzaGate conspiracy theory, powerful Democratic leaders—from Hillary Clinton to John Podesta—were running a child sex-trafficking ring out of the basement of Comet Ping Pong. Welch had been following the websites, social media accounts, and online forums propagating the PizzaGate conspiracy. As he went further down the conspiratorial rabbit hole, Welch became convinced that something evil was afoot at Comet Ping Pong. He felt morally obligated to investigate. So, on the morning of December 4, Welch left his wife and two daughters to drive the 350 miles to Washington from his home in North Carolina. Welch was determined to rescue the children being trafficked in the basement of the pizza restaurant.

As Welch later told the *New York Times*, his "heart [was] breaking over the thought of innocent people suffering."

After Welch's initial shots, the customers and employees of Comet Ping Pong fled the building. Welch commenced searching for the basement and other hidden rooms where the children were being imprisoned. But after forcing his way through the single locked door in the building, Welch discovered the simple, obvious, and fundamental flaw in the PizzaGate conspiracy theory: Comet Ping Pong didn't have a basement. There were no children. As Welch later concluded, "The intel on this wasn't 100%." Welch surrendered to the police when they arrived.

What happened to Edgar Welch would be darkly comical if it weren't for the fact that PizzaGate later morphed into QAnon, the conspiracy theory that fueled the attack on the US Capitol on January 6, 2021. The fact that Comet Ping Pong didn't have a basement did little to dissuade the conspiracy theorists that Democratic elites and deep-state operatives were working in the shadows to destroy America and hurt children. Conspiracy theories aren't so easily dislodged from the minds of true believers. Pointing out obvious facts—"Comet Ping Pong doesn't have a basement"—does little good. In fact, PizzaGate hasn't gone away and has recently become popular among young TikTok users.

Why are conspiracy theories so popular?

Psychologists have observed that conspiracy theories satisfy three human needs. The first need is epistemic, making sense of the world. The world is scary and unpredictable. By giving us a grand narrative of life, especially explanations for disconcerting and troubling events, conspiracy theories make life feel more coherent. Conspiracies proliferate because we prefer comforting lies over the unexplainable and mysterious. Answers and explanations are like cognitive security blankets, and conspiracy theories provide us with plenty.

Beyond epistemic needs, conspiracy theories also meet social needs. Conspiracy theories create community. Facing the ridicule of society and family members, conspiracy theorists band together, circling the wagons to create an "us against the world" network of support. A friend of mine whose parents became followers of QAnon shared with me how she had tried to confront them about what seemed to be obvious madness. She said that the pushback she got from her mom and dad had little to do with truth and reality. Facts really weren't the issue. The allure of QAnon was mainly *social*. "We've made some of the best friends of our lives," they said.

There is a third and final aspect of conspiracy theories I want us to focus on. Beyond satisfying epistemic and social needs, conspiracy theories satisfy existential needs, our hunger for meaning and significance in life. Like Edgar Welch, we all want to be a hero. Conspiracy theories typically see the world as a battle between good and evil. In this war, the conspiracy theorist enlists to join the army of light, working with others to save the world from cataclysmic destruction. Conspiracy theories are often crusades of righteousness. This narrative imbues life with sacred purpose and significance. Conspiracy theories are existential narcotics, intoxicating us with delusions of grandeur. In fact, "taking the red pill" is how QAnon adherents describe their conversion experience. Taken from the movie *The Matrix*—where the character Morpheus offers Neo a choice between a red pill, which will open his eyes to the truth, and a blue pill, which will keep him stuck in ordinary but illusory reality—QAnon describes true believers as "red pilled." Taking the red pill, diving deep into and embracing the QAnon worldview, opens your eyes to the truth. Like Neo in *The Matrix*, you enlist in the battle against evil. This is an intoxicating proposition. No longer are you working a dead-end job, living in the basement of your parents' house. Take the red pill, and you're now a soldier on the frontlines of a war. This heroic vision of yourself is an emotional high that's hard to find anywhere else.

The existential intoxication we observe in conspiracy theories parallels pathologies we also find among religious groups. For example, Christian apocalypticism, seen most especially among American fundamentalists and evangelicals, also satisfies epistemic, social, and existential needs. In many ways, QAnon can be seen as a secular version of Christian end-time beliefs, explaining why many evangelical Christians were among the January 6 insurrectionists. As with conspiracy theories, Christian apocalypticism invites us to play the hero.

As recounted in his book *American Apocalypse: A History of Modern Evangelicalism*, Matthew Sutton describes how the expectation of Christ's immanent return to establish a "millennial" reign on earth has characterized American Christianity from its earliest days. In trying to pinpoint the exact date of Jesus's second coming, fundamentalists and evangelicals have turned to prophetic texts in the Bible to interpret world history and current geopolitical events. Similar to conspiracy theories, these apocalyptic narratives describe a Manichean struggle between good and evil. To be sure, while the forces of the antichrist have changed with each generation—communism during the Cold War, Islam after the 9/11 attacks, and child-trafficking Democrats with QAnon—the pressing imperative was always the same: Christ's faithful were called to heroic action in a battle being waged against the demonic forces of evil.

Generation after generation, these end-time beliefs among Christians have met the same psychological needs as conspiracy theories. Biblical prophecy helps make sense of a world that is scary and unpredictable. As Sutton observes, American "apocalypticism provided radical evangelicals with a framework through which to interpret their lives, their communities, and the future. . . . It filled in blanks, rationalized choices, and connected dots." End-time beliefs also satisfy our need for the heroic. As Sutton continues, describing the origins and sustaining allure of apocalypticism among American evangelicals:

Whether driven by innately cynical dispositions, challenging personal circumstances, or simple restlessness, a handful of Christians from all regions, classes, levels of education, and walks of life determined that they were living in a shallow and meaningless age. Grasping newspapers in one hand and the prophetic books of the Bible in the other, they looked for encompassing solutions to their own—and the world's—problems. They found one in the resurrection and reconstitution of an ancient Christian tradition of millennialism. Following the lead of past generations of Christians, they used the Bible to decode history. Their sacred text provided them with secret knowledge of ages past, present, and to come. Their faith fostered a powerful sense of purpose and personal identity. . . . It offered them the promise of transformation and redemption in a world that seemed void of both. It also served as a call to battle.

The existential drug here is the same one that intoxicated Edgar Welch and the Capitol Hill insurrectionists. In a shallow and meaningless age infused with status anxiety, here is the red pill that will imbue your life with heroic purpose. Conspiracy theories and evangelical apocalypticism push the same drug. Take the pill, and your boring, low-status life becomes infused with world-historical significance. A battle is raging, and you've been called to war.

In 2010, an article in the *Seattle Post-Intelligencer* opened with the line "Vigilante justice has come to Seattle, and the caped crusaders drive a Kia." The article, entitled "Police Alerted to 'Superheroes' Patrolling Seattle," was one of the first to report on a fascinating season in the city of Seattle. Citizens of Seattle had begun dressing up as superheroes—complete with masks, capes, and names like Green Reaper, Gemini, Catastrophe, Thunder 88, and Phoenix Jones—to patrol the city streets and fight crime. Real-life Batmen and Robins. The superhero season was a zany time for the Rainy City and is wonderfully documented by journalist David Weinberg in the popular podcast *The Superhero Complex*.

Who were these real-life superheroes, and what were they up to? The website of the Rain City Superheroes shared their vision: "A Real Life Superhero is whoever chooses to embody the values presented in super heroic comic books, not only by donning a mask/costume, but also performing good deeds for the communitarian place whom he inhabits." This was more than cosplay and adults playing dress-up. The Real Life Superheroes were actually trying to be heroes. True, they didn't possess any superpowers to stop criminals. But their mere presence on the streets, standing around dressed like Superman, could deter crime. I know I'd keep my distance. And the Real Life Superheroes could quickly call the police if something criminal was observed. Also, many of the Seattle superheroes focused less on crime than on outreach to homeless people, handing out food and clothing to those in need. Which makes you wonder: Why would anyone need to put on spandex to hand out peanut butter and jelly sandwiches?

In his 1973 Pulitzer Prize–winning book, *The Denial of Death*, the anthropologist and psychologist Ernest Becker described the origin of the "the superhero complex." Specifically, contemporary life faces an existential vacuum. The philosopher Friedrich Nietzsche famously ushered in the modern world with his declaration that "God is dead." Without God, without some transcendent source of value and meaning, the modern self enters a world devoid of purpose. The atheist Richard Dawkins describes the world without God this way: "In a universe of blind physical forces and genetic replication, some people are going to get hurt, other people are going to get lucky, and you won't find any rhyme or reason in it, nor any justice. The universe we observe has precisely the properties we should expect if there is, at bottom, no design, no purpose, no evil and no good, nothing but blind, pitiless indifference."

This pitiless cosmos where life has "no purpose" creates a psychological crisis. Because we want our lives to matter. We want our small acts of kindness and compassion to carry some significance. We want our sacrifices to count in some larger, cosmic sense. Facing this predicament, says Becker, we search for a means of significance. We do this by creating and participating in a "hero system," which I describe to my students as a *hero game*. We play this hero game, in the words of Becker, "to earn a feeling of primary value," a sense of cosmic specialness. This hero game makes us matter and count. Winning our hero game is how we achieve self-esteem.

Simply stated, everyone has a superhero complex. We all want to matter, so we each invent some game of significance that we can "win." Sometimes these hero games are ludicrous, like dressing up like Batman. And sometimes they are dangerous, like walking into a pizza shop with an assault rifle. Sometimes these games are religious, like predicting the end-times and identifying some world leader as the antichrist. And sometimes these games are nonreligious, like the QAnon believers taking their red pills. But whoever you are, and this is crucial to understand, you are playing a hero game.

When the modern self collapsed, self-esteem became entangled in the superhero complex. Like Edgar Welch and Seattle's caped crusaders, most of us want to be a hero. We want to live a meaningful and significant life. So we play a game of significance. Of course, your game is different from my game, but we're both trying to win at something. You don't need to wear a cape to have a superhero complex. Consider the pathologies of fan culture.

In 2013, the video game developer Zoë Quinn endured death threats and vitriol for attempting to introduce feminist content and themes into the male-dominated gaming world. The harassment endured by Quinn became known as Gamergate, described by Wikipedia as an "organized misogynistic online harassment campaign and a right-wing backlash against feminism, diversity, and progressivism in video game culture." Quinn, and other women who became targets of the harassment campaign, faced doxing, death threats, and rape threats. Gamers shared nude photos of the targeted women with their work colleagues and hacked the accounts of their family and friends. Someone called Quinn's father to call her a "whore." As Quinn shared at a gaming conference, "I used to go to game events and feel like I was going home. . . . Now it's just like . . . are any of the people I'm currently in the room with ones that said they wanted to beat me to death?" All this hate and bile over *video games*.

As another example, look at the harassment and blowback that Rian Johnson received for writing and directing the movie *The Last Jedi*. Hardcore fans of the Star Wars franchise were furious with Johnson for how his movie attempted to displace the Skywalker family from the center of the Star Wars universe and "democratize" the Force. In prior Star Wars lore, only the special few—like the Skywalker clan—could use the quasi-mystical powers of the Force. Fan fury turned into online harassment, causing

Johnson to observe, "Before I made *The Last Jedi*, I had never had anyone hate me on the internet."

There seems to be an asymmetry here between the magnitude of the hatred given the triviality of the subject matter. From video games to movie franchises, what is behind the violent and vitriolic reactions we observe within fan culture? Author and essayist Freddie deBoer follows in the footsteps of Ernest Becker in describing these pathologies of fan culture. Specifically, deBoer points to how the collapse of meaning in the modern world created new challenges in becoming and establishing the value of the self. Into this void stepped capitalism, which began to provide us, through its various products and entertainments, with a way to buy or borrow an identity. As deBoer observes, "If you can't generate real meaning and psychological security in your life, Amazon would be more than happy to sell it to you." DeBoer goes on to describe how many of these products, like movies and video games, traffic in stories and how stories carry meaning. This is a potent and addictive cocktail for selves searching for purpose. We can *borrow* meaning by *inhabiting* the fictitious stories being sold to us, from Harry Potter to Star Wars. "Unfortunately," says deBoer, "this can have the effect of fooling oneself into thinking that consuming these representations of meaning is the same thing as having meaning, of feeling one has a meaning-driven life." Through imaginative identification, fan culture tricks us into thinking we're living a heroic life. Lacking a story of my own, I can rent one from my favorite video game or movie.

The superhero complex explains why video game and Star Wars fans are pushed into violent hysterics when their beloved products and franchises get disturbed. Video games and movies have become *repositories of meaning*, wrapped up into our hero games. Fans make death threats because the video game or movie is more than a bit of fun entertainment. Movies and games are bike pumps being used to reinflate the deflated ego, a means to imbue life with purpose, weight, and significance. That the superhero complex we observe in fan culture is totally pathological and dysfunctional brings deBoer to his stinging conclusion:

> I think a lot of nerds have fallen into the trap of thinking that liking Marvel movies is a personality. They have steeped themselves so fully inside these products that they have come to think of them when they think of themselves. "I love it so much, it must be me." And this is a mistake. Liking Star Wars simply isn't a solid foundation for your personality; the human psyche needs more fundamental codes and commitments to work with. Star Wars isn't in your control, so if you give yourself up to it and someone does something with it that you don't like, your whole world gets rocked. Ask the people who hated *The Last Jedi*. And these properties, no matter how sophisticated they are, or how beloved they are, just can't contain enough substance to anchor a sense of self.

In 2014, Sucy Park was a loud and proud social media activist. As an Asian American woman of color, Park was an antiracist force on Twitter, calling out oppression with hashtags that skyrocketed up Twitter's trending list. Park's hashtag #NotYourAsianSidekick drew media attention and accolades for effectively calling out Asian stereotypes in popular culture. Things were going well; the cause was being advanced. Then Park made a fatal mistake. She called out Stephen Colbert.

On March 26 of that year, Colbert was still hosting his Comedy Central show *The Colbert Report*, where he satirically played the character of a rightwing TV pundit. In the guise of his character, a character who was overtly sexist and racist in order to poke fun at sexists and racists, Colbert took to the show's Twitter account to announce, "I am willing to show #Asian community I care by introducing the Ching-Chong Ding-Dong Foundation for Sensitivity to Orientals or Whatever." Colbert's tweet was mocking the NFL's Washington Redskins, who had just announced the creation of a charitable foundation in the hope that it would draw attention away from the controversy brewing about its use of an objectionable term for Indigenous Americans for its team mascot. (In 2022, the Redskins became the Washington Commanders.) Suey Park, however, didn't find anything funny about Colbert's use of satire. In response, Park tweeted, "The Ching-Chong Ding-Dong Foundation for Sensitivity to Orientals has decided to call for #CancelColbert. Trend it."

The hashtag #CancelColbert went viral, rocketing to the top of Twitter's trending list. Political pundits on the right, who had long been skewered by Colbert's show, howled with glee to see Colbert get his comeuppance, called out by social justice warriors and facing potential cancellation. But the backlash soon shifted. Beloved by the political left, Colbert was not an easy target to take down. Suey Park began to face her own cancellation from former allies and fans on the left. Once a darling of social media activism, Park became the object of scorn and hate. The political left had, as it often can, turned on one of its own. An article in the *New Republic* entitled "Why Won't Twitter Forgive Suey Park?" documented the fallout: "Petitions about Park began to appear on Change.org, including one that demanded she be removed 'as an Asian American representative.' On Reddit, users skewered her as 'totally f**king racist,' 'a piece of sh*t,' and fantasized about her being stabbed and beaten. On 4chan and its offshoots, people attempted to figure out where she lived and worked. She grew concerned enough about her safety that she began canceling speaking appearances. 'I lost my income. I wasn't safe,' Park said. 'It was scary. Really scary.'"

We didn't have a word for it then, but since 2014, we've all become intimately familiar with the toxicity of callout and cancel culture. Online activism has become a hero game, a game we can win or lose. We call this game *performative activism* or *virtue signaling*. Generally played by the political left, the goal of the game is to always be on the right side of the oppressor/oppressed dichotomy. Playing this game successfully, always correctly calling out and canceling the oppressors, imbues life with moral purpose and significance. We're soldiers in a war being fought one hashtag at a time.

Playing this game can be a risky, high-stakes poker game. No one wants their social media activity to get tagged as "problematic." But the tables can turn on anyone. Even a woman of color like Suey Park can get burned. Social media giveth, and social media taketh away. Twitter (now called X by its new owner, Elon Musk) can be a cruel and unforgiving master. And once you've been excommunicated and canceled, rehabilitation is practically impossible.

Political activism has its own issues with the superhero complex, a hero game where we escalate our solidarity with the oppressed by calling out those less committed to the cause. Radical movements eventually come to eat their own as they play this game of moral one-upmanship. Our heroic quest for a meaningful life causes us to burn the house down, even if friends and allies are inside. Just ask Bernardine Dohrn.

Bernardine Dohrn was the (in)famous leader of the Weather Underground, the radical leftist group that conducted a domestic terror campaign in the United States, bombing buildings to protest racism and the Vietnam War. After years of living underground under a false identity to avoid the FBI, Dohrn was eventually forced by her own people, because she wanted to marry and have children, to publicly record and share a confession about being complicit in the patriarchy. Wanting to have a family was too bourgeoisie, too self-indulgent given the sacrifices the revolution demanded. Ponder the irony. Bernardine Dohrn had *bombed buildings* and was *hunted by the FBI*, only the second woman to ever appear on the FBI's America's Most Wanted List. But that wasn't radical enough. Dohrn had failed the revolution because she wanted to be a mom. This is the inexorable logic of the superhero complex at work in social justice activism, pushing radical activists to cannibalize their own and political causes into escalating violence.

In her interview with the *New Republic*, Suey Park described the dysfunctions of radical activism, how the hero game of leftist Twitter closely resembles the "purity culture" decried within evangelical Christianity: "Park's understanding of her Twitter presence carries a distinctly Christian note. 'It's a lot like purity politics in the church,' Park observed, referring to the tendency of Twitter groups to attack perceived wrongdoers. It is, she pointed out, a strategy that works for activists until it turns on them. 'You do one wrong thing,' Park said, 'and you're tainted. You're out forever.'"

No one is immune to these political hero games. The political left and right each has its own superhero complexes. Politics is, perhaps, the biggest hero game being played in the world right now. Consider how political psychologists have been tracking the rise of *affective polarization*. Different from issue polarization, where we disagree about how best to solve the problems facing our countries, affective polarization has to do with the negative feelings we have about people who vote differently than we do. Measures of affective polarization assess the increasingly hostile feelings Democrats have for Republicans and Republicans for Democrats. As we all have witnessed, our politics have become increasingly bitter and hate-filled. Our political debates are no longer principled disagreements between fellow citizens but bomb-throwing between sworn enemies. Politics has become a fight between good and evil, our modern, secular form of holy war.

The comparison between politics and religion is appropriate. Research has shown that we now identify more strongly with our political party than with our religion, race, or nation. Our strongest impulses to discriminate are no longer directed at racial or religious differences but at political opponents. Politics has become for us the ultimate hero game, the repository of our most deeply held values and beliefs. Nothing defines the modern self better than how we vote. The existential weight of politics escalates affective polarization. Political disagreements are no longer pragmatic attempts to solve problems but are, rather, experienced as a rejection of my most cherished convictions, a denial of my very self. And the deeper the cut, the more violent the defensive response. Politics has become a blood sport because it means too much, not politically but *psychologically*. Every election, my *identity* is on the ballot. Are you for *me* or against *me*?

Hero games are insidious. As Michael Corleone says in *The God-father 3*, "Just when I thought I was out, they pull me back in!"

I remember when I got the invitation to write my first book. Publishing a book is a huge part of winning the hero game of being a college professor. I had ambitions to write a book, like all professors do, but after ten years of teaching in anonymity, I didn't know if I would ever get the chance. But one day, I got an invitation. I fondly recall the day copies of my book arrived in the mail, a memorable moment for all first-time authors. Finally, I had done it! I'd published a book. I'd arrived. I had won.

But then a funny thing happened. Just when I had settled into my season of success, people started asking me, "How's your book selling?" The questions made me insecure. I was proud of the book, but it wasn't rocketing up the bestseller lists. I soon developed a bad habit of regularly checking the book's Amazon sales ranking, watching it get lower and lower and lower. Each time I checked on the sales, my self-image took a hit. I also began to notice feelings of jealousy and envy toward other authors. I resented their popularity, their glowing reviews, huge sales, and landing on the *New York Times* bestseller list. I grumbled darkly to myself, "That book isn't all that great. Mine is better."

Things got worse. Beyond sales, reader reviews started to appear on Amazon and Goodreads. Now, I will humbly, or insecurely, confess that all my books have received very good reviews. But as an author, you don't pay attention to that. What stings in the midst of a hundred glowing reviews is a single negative review. Sadly, our brains are more attuned to negative feedback than to positive. We quickly forget twenty compliments to obsess over one criticism. This makes reading your book reviews a nightmare. You ignore the praise and fixate on the trolls. Currently, one of my books has a 4.27 out of 5 rating on Goodreads. Which is great. But the tragedy is that I don't think about that; what I think about is a review like this one from Victoria Weinstein:

> This is a plodding, dull approach to a fascinating subject. Beck's sentence structure is repetitive and pedantic and his tone is that of a youth minister lecturing to a group of 8th graders . . . BORING. He relies on italics to enliven his prose, but it doesn't help. . . .
>
> Don't bother with this one unless you are a youth minister, in which case I think it might be a good resource.

Ouch. Beyond Victoria's very low opinion of youth ministers, she's definitely not a fan of my writing. For an author, a review like this can get into your head.

Here is what I discovered when I published a book. I had stepped out of one hero game right into another. I'd won the *professor* hero game by finally getting published. A win! But I quickly discovered I'd started playing the *author* hero game, a game governed by bestseller lists, book reviews, and sales rankings. I thought I had won, only to realize I was losing all over again.

I've been talking about a lot of different hero games in this chapter—from politics to conspiracy theories to religion to activism to video gamers. Maybe you've been caught up in some of these games. But most of our hero games are personal and unique. Not a huge game involving thousands but the game I've chosen for my own life. These are the games we play in our workplaces or gyms. Among friends who share a hobby or common interest. We compare how much weight we can lift at the bench press or how much weight we've lost on the scale. We note who gets promoted at work and who doesn't. Maybe we're into gardening or our whiskey collection. Maybe we have a fashion sense, have followers on Twitter, or have the best taste in music. Maybe you are creative and an artist. Perhaps you're good at Wordle or dominate your fantasy football league. As I tell my students, "Everybody is a snob about something." We all have something we cherish, where we are considered the best, can show off, or stand in the spotlight as the expert in the room. We all have a game we're playing.

Our families of origin have hero games as well. Every family instills in you a vision of what a "winning" life looks like. Maybe it's financial success and ski vacations in Colorado. Perhaps it's captured in the big family portrait on the beach with everyone wearing matching white shirts and khaki pants. Maybe it's going to college, getting married, and having kids. The approval of our parents is the scorecard of this game, our successes and failures measured in Mom and Dad's disappointment with how we've turned out. It's the hero game tracked by the resentments of sibling rivalries and facing our inadequacies every holiday and family reunion.

When you play these games of status, success, and significance, you measure winning and losing by what psychologists call upward and downward social comparison. Feelings of snobbery, superiority, and vanity—"winning" our hero game—flow out of downward social comparison as we look down on those beneath our level of attainment. Feelings of "losing" our hero game involve emotions of envy and jealousy, judgments of upward social comparison, the resentments and shame we feel witnessing the success of others.

In a world sick with status anxiety, upward and downward social comparison infuses every social interaction with the potential for diminishment. How will I compare with you when we meet? Will your life successes fill me with a gnawing sense of jealousy? Or will I bask in the glow of smug superiority as I share with you my latest accomplishment?

If all this sounds like a miserable way to go through life, it is. But hero games are our addiction. Status is a drug. For example, one of the worst-received talks I ever delivered was at a retreat for powerful and successful young Christian professionals, a selective and handpicked group deemed to be future "difference makers" in the world. The speaker before me had called this high-achieving group of young professionals into practices of Sabbath and rest. This message fell on the audience like rain in the desert, as it does in just about every church and organization. "Rest!" we exclaim. "I need that." Life is so busy and stressful. We all need to slow down, to unplug and restore ourselves. We crave seasons of Sabbath. And yet few of us actually practice Sabbath. We never slow down. It's a puzzle: Why do we avoid doing what we desire so much? Why won't we rest?

When I got up to speak to the young professionals, I shared the answer. "The reason we don't rest," I explained, "is because of shame. It takes shame resiliency to practice Sabbath." It all goes back to our hero games. Remember, scarcity is a whack-a-mole problem. Our hero games get us caught up in scarcity traps, where investment in one area of life demands a divestment elsewhere. "For example," I shared with the professionals, "say you want to be a better father. If so, you have to face the fact that while you're coaching your child's Little League game on Saturday, your business competitor, either inside or outside your company, will be in the office outworking you." This is, let's admit, a fairly obvious observation about resource allocation. More *here* means less *there*. Simple math. But I had just slapped my audience in the face. I had burst the delusion behind their hero game. I pushed on:

> If you start stepping away from work to practice Sabbath or to invest in being a better spouse or parent, you'll start falling behind at work compared with others. Your rivals will advance beyond you. They'll get the promotion. Because they are *working* while you're *resting*, coaching Little League or making pancakes for your kids on Saturday morning. That is the hard truth. If you want to practice Sabbath, you will have to get used to losing at something. You'll have to face the shame of falling behind in some game of success you're currently playing to step into a different, healthier rhythm of life.

Like I said, this talk didn't go over very well. I had challenged the superhero complex of this very successful, high-achieving, and driven group, the game that was defining their self-image and pursuit of significance. A young VP from Goldman Sachs angrily cornered my wife after the talk to share with her some choice insults directed at me. I don't expect to be invited back.

I share this story simply to say that it's not easy to step away from your hero game. Even when the game is killing you. Or killing your family. The metaphor of addiction really does fit here. We cling to the source of our self-esteem, the fount of our value and worth, like a security blanket. Because without the game, we're nothing. We'd rather burn out, destroy our health, and ruin our families than let go of what makes us worthy of someone's time and attention. This is the sickness at the heart of the modern self, the psychological cancer of the superhero complex.

Like inflating a car tire with a bike pump, our hero games deplete us. But I wonder if you've noticed something other than weariness that has been haunting us.

Beyond the exhaustion of the superhero complex, all the ways we try to fight off failure and shame, there's a dark thread that has run through every hero game we've talked about. Our hero games do more than exhaust; these games are also contrastive, comparative, and competitive. They are games, after all. Many of our hero games involve an us-versus-them conflict. Some of these are games of good versus evil, like we see in political, conspiracy theory, religious, and activist hero games. Or they are games of insiders versus outsiders, like what we observe with fan culture freak-outs. Other hero games get caught up in downward versus upward comparison, hero games of winning versus losing in relation to others. This is the game where I monitor my book sales and obsess over bad reviews, the hero games of envy, jealousy, insecurity, and shame. Hero games of achievement, burnout, perfectionism, entitlement, workaholism, vanity, selfishness, and pride.

Here's the sad and tragic truth about the superhero complex. It's not just that self-esteem is exhausting. Self-esteem is an act of aggression. Self-esteem is *agonistic*, rooted in competitive games of comparison. Our hero games embed us in *neurotic rivalries*, a running scoreboard in our minds keeping track of how well we are doing in relation to others. Emotional health is not just about learning how to *rest*, how to step away from the bike pump. Wholeness is stepping into *peace*. And by *peace*, I don't just mean calm. I mean *nonviolent*; I mean stepping away from a competitive and comparative way of achieving meaning and significance in your life. This is a peace that can only come by letting go of our addiction to "win" or "be the best" at something, to hit some mark we've set for ourselves—the rest of stepping away from envy and jealousy when we're at the bottom and vanity and narcissism when we're at the top. Joy begins with renouncing the game, throwing both downward and upward comparison into the trash.

Bestselling author Will Storr describes the superhero complex as a ubiquitous and never-ending "status game" of rivalry and competition fueled by the emotion of resentment. Storr calls this resentment "the universal prejudice" and fingers this hostility as the cause of much of the misery in the world. Storr observes in his book *The Status Game*, "The resentments [our status games] trigger can sour the story we tell of the world, populating it with a ceaseless line-up of villains at whom we point and jeer and sing our songs of derision in all our righteousness and envy." The universal prejudice of the superhero complex, says Storr, "is responsible for much of the misery, anxiety and exhaustion we experience. . . . It certainly causes a lot of the hostility we feel towards others."

Our self-images are entangled in conflict. And if it's not a violence directed outwardly, toward people we envy, despise, or damn, we turn the knives on ourselves. We lacerate our souls with self-loathing. Feeling that we are failures and losers, we can't live at peace with ourselves.

Here, we come face to face with the tragic legacy of the modern self. This is the darkness that haunts our hero games— a universal prejudice. Hating—others or yourself—is the dark shadow of the superhero complex.

Time, now, to hold up the mirror.

I have few questions to ask you: What's your hero game? How are you exhausting yourself pursing status, success, and significance? Why can't *you* rest? What bike pump of self-esteem are you working at so furiously to fill your life with purpose? Where are you seeing the devil in the face of others? What are the prejudices at the root of your easy hatreds?

I know you (probably) aren't wearing a cape or a mask, but tell me: What's your superhero complex?

Part 2

TURNING AWAY

4 | TURN DOWN THE VOLUME

Last summer, I spent a week of spiritual retreat in France with the Taizé community. Founded by Brother Roger Schütz in 1949, Taizé is an ecumenical monastic community. Today, Taizé's mission is largely directed at young people, though adults can take a retreat there during select times of the year. Taizé is famous around the world for its distinctive music—haunting, meditative, and chantlike songs.

A retreat at Taizé is organized around joining the brothers three times a day for their morning, afternoon, and evening prayer services. The experience is contemplative. You are asked to enter the Church of Reconciliation in silence. There are no seats or pews. You kneel or sit on the floor through the service. Thankfully, there are prayer stools available to help us older folks keep some weight off our knees. The services are centered on singing the songs composed by Taizé, along with Scripture readings in different languages. And at each service, there is a ten-minute period of silence.

Now, you might think ten minutes isn't all that long to sit in silence. But if you've ever practiced contemplative prayer or sitting meditation, you know ten minutes of silence can feel like an eternity. And during my time at Taizé, I was doing this three times a day for an entire week.

My first day at Taizé was a mental battle. Each time we stepped into the silence, my mind exploded with noise. I couldn't get my thoughts to settle down. My mind wandered. I mentally observed myself trying to "be contemplative" as I knelt. I began to judge myself for my inability to maintain a prayerful focus. My mind was like flypaper. Every time I touched a thought, I got stuck in the glue. I struggled to extract myself by thinking more thoughts, but that only deepened my inner anxious spiral. I couldn't shake free.

As I'm sure you know, your mind is a very noisy place.

When the self collapsed in on itself, it raised an interesting question. What happens when the mind is left all alone, like a prisoner sitting in solitary confinement? Having turned inward, away from external stimuli, maybe the mind would grow quiet, sitting patiently and still as it waited for something interesting in the world to come knocking on the doors of consciousness. Sadly, that isn't what happens. As I experienced my first day Taizé, try to sit quietly, and you'll come face to face with a boil of thoughts within yourself. Turing inward, you won't experience peaceful, quiet bliss. What you'll find are jumpy, scattered thoughts.

Neuroscientists and psychologists have discovered that the "default state" of the brain, what the brain is doing when you're not doing anything, is a "wandering mind." Our minds don't sit still and quiet. We leap from thought to thought like a frog in a frying pan. And the story here is even worse than you think. This chronic mental wandering negatively affects our mental health. For example, a 2010 study published in *Science* followed over five thousand people with a smartphone app that randomly contacted the participants during the day. When contacted, the app asked the person what they were doing at that moment, along with this question "Are you thinking about something other than what you are currently doing?" Basically, is your mind wandering right now? Not surprisingly, the study found that our minds wander *a lot*. In 46.9 percent of the cases, the participants reported that their minds were wandering at that moment. Ponder that. Almost half of our waking lives are spent lost within ourselves. Mentally, we're just not present; we're somewhere else. And here's the most tragic finding of the study: mental wandering was associated with increased unhappiness. As the researchers concluded, "a wandering mind is an unhappy mind."

Put these findings together and you have a recipe for widespread misery. Our default mental state is that our minds wander, and getting lost within ourselves makes us unhappy. Emotional unrest is the consequence of being curved inward upon yourself. Our minds have become haunted houses with our thoughts gloomily wandering their lonely corridors like ghosts.

Most of our mental wandering takes the shape of self-talk, a voice in our heads. The ego is talkative and chatty, keeping up a running commentary throughout the day. Much of our unhappiness stems from paying more attention to this inner voice than to what is happing in the world around us. Our attention is bent inward. We miss out on life because we're morbidly self-focused.

The running commentary we hear rattling around inside our skulls tends to be reports about our superhero complex, how we're winning or losing the game of self-esteem. Like NFL broadcasters on *Monday Night Football*, we hear in our minds a constant stream of play-by-play commentary about how well we're performing. We're at a social gathering talking with others, barely paying attention because we're so focused on the voice in our heads castigating us for some social slip up we've just committed: "Oh no! She called him John, and his name is Phil. Awkward! Folks, we don't know how she's ever going to dig herself out of this hole." On the outside, we're smiling and nodding along, but on the inside, we're listening to news reports of our social failure.

The psychologist Ethan Kross calls this negative inner dialogue "chatter," and his research has explored how this inner voice is ruining our lives. Kross describes in his book *Chatter: The Voice in Our Head, Why It Matters, and How to Harness It* what I've already shared with you: Sigmund Freud gave us very bad advice about where to find happiness. As Kross notes, Freud argued that "'going inside' was the route to a resilient, fulfilling life." But what we discovered inside ourselves has made us profoundly unhappy and unwell. Psychologists are only just now beginning to pick up the pieces caused by following Freud into the caverns of our minds in the hope of uncovering treasures of peace and bliss. Kross describes what science has discovered about this search: "In recent years, a robust body of new research has demonstrated that *when we experience distress, engaging in introspection often does significantly more harm than good*. It undermines our performance at work, interferes with our ability to make good decisions, and negatively influences our relationships. It can also promote violence and aggression, contribute to a range of mental disorders, and enhance our risk of becoming physically ill" (italics mine).

Turning inward doesn't produce joy; it produces depression, anxiety, and hostility. You won't find rest by "going inside" yourself. Cut off from the world, your mind will slowly poison itself.

If joy has a shape, we have to flip the self inside out, from being curved inward to being curved outward. You need to reverse the curvature of your ego. And the first step in this process is *turning away* from your internal chatter. Here in part 2, I'll show you how to do this. Let's take a step back from our wandering, unhappy minds.

But this raises a question: What does it look like to "turn away" from myself? As I've pictured this, I've come to think of our ego—the *you* inside your head—as a six-sided hexagon. Each of the sides of this honeycomb is a window on the self. These six aspects of the ego overlap a bit, but they are distinct enough to talk about separately. Taken together, the honeycomb brings into view the sort of ego we should strive for to avoid the pathologies of modern life—the trap of self-esteem, the superhero complex, our wandering minds, and the chattering voice in our heads. Here is the honeycomb model of the ego, with its six windows on the self:

Let's start at the top with ego volume.

As I struggled in the silences of Taizé, I faced what psychologists call "ego volume." Your mind can be either quiet or noisy. When your ego is loud, the chatter in your head is intrusive and disruptive. The volume of this inner noise drags your attention inward. When ego volume is loud, the self collapses. You're pulled out of life and back into your head.

In contrast to a noisy ego, ego volume is turned down by cultivating a quiet ego. With a quiet ego, your inner voice takes a break. The chatter lessens. Obsessive self-absorption wanes. A quiet ego allows you to turn away from yourself, returning your attention to the world and others. You become emotionally, physically, and mentally present.

Your ego volume affects your joy. Research has found that a quieter ego is associated with increased self-esteem, greater life satisfaction, happiness, psychological resilience, and greater meaning in life. The science is clear: we need to turn down the volume.

During the 1950s and '60s, Dr. Aaron Beck was growing increasingly disillusioned. Beck had trained as a psychoanalyst, steeping himself in the theories and techniques of Sigmund Freud. Following the dictates of psychoanalytic theory, Beck was asking his depressed patients to turn inward, to become more deeply introspective. This deep dive into themselves was expected to lead Beck's patients toward joy.

But that's not what Aaron Beck was observing in his therapeutic practice. As a good psychoanalyst, Beck turned his patients inward, but they kept getting stuck within themselves. Beck's depressed clients drowned in their memories and ruminations, unable to come up for air. "Going inside" wasn't making Beck's clients happier; it was making them more depressed.

Turns out, one of the most toxic things for our mental health is what psychologists call *depressive rumination*. Depressive rumination occurs when our thoughts fixate on, attach to, and swirl around some loss, fear, wound, failure, shame, hurt, or inadequacy. When we ruminate, we pick at our emotional scabs, never allowing them to heal.

What Aaron Beck noticed early in his counseling career was that Freud's theory of going inside was exacerbating depressive rumination among his clients. Instead of letting emotional wounds heal, Freudian introspection kept them bleeding. Beck eventually concluded that what his clients needed was *to step away* from their thoughts in order to adopt a more critical and objective perspective on their internal chatter. Beck called this stepping back *distancing*, and it became a vital part of his new approach to treating depression. In one of the most pivotal moments in modern psychological history, Aaron Beck left Freud behind to become the founder of what would later become cognitive-behavioral therapy (CBT).

Aaron Beck passed away in 2021, and as the founder of CBT, he is arguably the most famous and influential psychiatrist since Sigmund Freud. Aaron Beck's CBT was the first psychological treatment to scientifically demonstrate clinical effectiveness across a wide range of mood, personality, and behavioral disorders. Because of this, CBT is now used to treat—well, just about everything. My doctoral research, for example, was one of the first published reviews demonstrating the effectiveness of CBT in the treatment of anger problems. Multiple studies have also compared CBT with antidepressant medication in the treatment of depression, demonstrating that CBT can be as effective, and often more effective, than taking pills. And all of this success is rooted in a very simple idea: take a step back from yourself.

As Aaron Beck observed with his early clients, we can turn down our ego volume by getting some distance from the voice in our heads. And you don't need CBT to experience these benefits. For example, research has shown a simple and effective way to disentangle yourself from your inner chatter: You can change your inner pronouns when you talk to yourself. Instead of using "I" in your inner dialogue, you can substitute your first name. Or switch from "I" to "you." Rather than thinking "What do I want?" I can practice thinking "What does Richard want?" Psychologists describe this technique as *self-distancing*, a simple tool that helps you gain a more objective view of yourself.

You can also practice self-distancing by talking to yourself like a friend. This "best friend technique" is a simple self-care recommendation used by just about every therapist in the world. When we're wrestling with hard decisions or struggling with negative emotions, rather than getting overwhelmed with a tidal wave of thoughts and feelings, can we stop and ask ourselves, "If my best friend were going through something like this, what would I say to them?" Using this technique, you become your own "best friend." Critical to this act of self-*compassion* is self-*distance*, stepping away from yourself to adopt a healthier perspective. Self-distancing techniques—changing your inner pronouns or talking to yourself like a friend—might seem trivial, but they are powerful tools in cultivating emotional health and resiliency.

Despite the dazzling successes of CBT, some psychologists in the 1980s and '90s came to feel that Aaron Beck didn't push his initial insight about distancing far enough. While Beck recommended that his clients step back from their depressive ruminations, he did ask them to reengage their thoughts through what is called *cognitive restructuring*, a technique used to break down and rebuild our inner self-talk. The process of cognitive restructuring involves attending to our thoughts in order to challenge and modify them when they are unhelpful or inaccurate. A central goal of CBT is to help clients replace dysfunctional and self-defeating thoughts with healthier thinking.

This makes sense, trying to shift our inner chatter into a more self-compassionate register. Your inner voice can be harsh or supportive, critical or caring. But psychologists from within the CBT community began to argue that the process of cognitive restructuring remains a type of rumination. CBT was still asking people to *focus on* and *engage with* their thinking. Yes, clients were being asked to engage their self-talk with more distance and objectivity, but CBT keeps you focusing on your thoughts. You've got to pay attention to negative thoughts if you want to change them. Perhaps CBT wasn't as distanced as it could be. Following that idea, the psychologist Steven Hayes pioneered what would become acceptance and commitment therapy (ACT). In contrast to CBT, ACT argues that, when it comes to our thinking, we need *comprehensive distancing*. Aaron Beck's original insight needed to be taken one step further.

We need comprehensive distancing because our thoughts really are like flypaper. Last summer, when we had some flies in the house, I grew weary of chasing them around with a flyswatter. I went to the store and bought some flypaper. The gooey, sticky paper came rolled up in a tube. I started to unroll the paper but made the mistake of touching the sticky part. I tried to shake free. But in shaking the paper, it hit the cabinet and got stuck. I instinctively reached up with my free hand to pull the paper off the cabinet. Now that hand was stuck. Unable to use either hand, I tried to shake both hands free at the same time. That caused the paper to stick to the countertop. The flypaper was now stuck to everything—both hands, the countertop, and the kitchen cabinet. This had seemed like a simple job, hanging up some flypaper, but in less than a minute, I'd succeeded in only trapping myself.

Our thoughts are just like this. The more you engage them, the more stuck you get. That was the argument made by the pioneers of ACT and acceptance-based treatments. As effective as CBT is, we're still engaging with our thoughts, still grabbing the flypaper. Acceptance-based approaches to mental health argue for something different: perhaps you shouldn't touch the flypaper at all.

Since the 1990s, acceptance-based approaches have become one of the influential movements in the field of psychotherapy. According to acceptance-based therapies, rather than monitoring and trying to change your thoughts—grabbing the flypaper— you are encouraged to sit back and merely observe your thoughts.

You don't engage your inner chatter; you simply note it and let it go. When we have negative thoughts, we simply accept that the thought is there. We don't try to talk back to it, change it, or remove it. We don't debate ourselves. We let the thoughts pass. Like clouds floating by. We refuse to grab the flypaper. Practicing this comprehensive distancing from the voice in our heads has proven to be remarkably effective. Since its introduction, ACT has shown itself to be as effective as CBT in treating mental and behavioral disorders and often outperforms CBT.

I've shared the history of CBT and the development of acceptance-based therapies to communicate two crucial insights to you. First, notice this: from CBT's distancing to the comprehensive distancing of acceptance-based approaches, two of the most effective and versatile psychotherapies in the world involve stepping away from your thoughts. I'll say it again: Freud was wrong. Chasing thoughts inside our heads isn't a recipe for happiness.

The second thing to notice is how mindfulness, through comprehensive distancing, is taking center stage in modern psychotherapies. Mindfulness is now widely considered to be one of the simplest and most effective techniques in our therapeutic and self-care toolkits.

Grounded in Eastern spiritual traditions, mindfulness involves practicing a nonjudgmental attention to the present moment. The simple practice of mindfulness meditation illustrates the point. Mindfulness meditation involves sitting quietly for a period of time and engaging in some focal practice, such as paying attention to your breathing. As you attend to your breath, you'll begin to experience what I experienced sitting in the silences of Taizé. You will come face to face with your noisy ego, all the internal chatter. Your mind will start to wander. Your attention will get drawn away from your breath. You'll think of something you have to get done. Or something you forgot to do. Random thoughts will intrude. You'll start up an internal dialogue, talking to yourself. You'll wonder how much time has passed. Critical to mindfulness practice, when you notice your mind racing off like this, is that you don't judge the mental wandering. You simply let go of the thoughts, noting them but patiently and nonjudgmentally returning your attention back toward your breathing. Starting off, this practice can be very difficult. But over time, it becomes easier to stay present and focused. The ego volume gets turned down. Your mind becomes practiced in quieting itself.

Beyond meditation, we can also practice mindfulness in daily life whenever we experience stressful or triggering situations. Stop where you are and take ten slow breaths, attending to your breathing. Beyond breathing, you can also become more mindful of your surroundings. Whenever you're getting caught up in your thoughts or overwhelmed by your feelings, stop and notice five things that you can see. Then notice five things you can hear. Then five things you are touching. Finally, try to notice all these things at once. Simple grounding techniques like this pull you out of your head and quiet your ego.

In the Western Christian tradition, there's a close connection between mindfulness and the practices of contemplative prayer. This is what I was doing at Taizé. To be sure, for many

Christians, prayer remains a noisy activity. We can talk a lot during prayer, either out loud or internally. The practices of contemplative prayer, by contrast, don't involve "talking" to God. Like mindfulness, contemplative prayer quiets the ego. Focus is often still directed on our breathing, with words of prayer repeated on breathing in and breathing out. The critical spiritual difference between mindfulness and contemplative prayer is the contrast between therapeutic technique and transcendent encounter. In contemplative prayer, we expect to meet a Presence in the quietness, a Voice of peace and love that is not my own. As Thomas Merton described it, "Contemplation is essentially a listening in silence, an expectancy." In quieting the ego, we listen for the "still small voice" at the center of our being, a voice that is impossible to hear with a noisy, scattered, and anxious mind.

Taizé came home with me to Texas. Icons from the monastery hang on my walls. I packed two prayer stools made by the monks into my carry-on luggage. Using the stools, one for home and one for my office, kneeling during prayer keeps me connected to the silence I experienced in France. As the days passed at the monastery, I began to look forward to the minutes of quiet during our prayer services. The monks of Taizé had taught my mind how to rest. I didn't want to lose those lessons when I got back to the States.

Our journey toward joy begins here in this silence, with the quieting of your ego. We start with the simplest of recommendations: Take a step back from yourself. Turn away from the chatter of your wandering mind. Don't grab the flypaper of your thoughts. Practice comprehensive self-distancing through practices of mindfulness and contemplative prayer. Let your mind learn to quiet itself. Take that volume knob attached to your ego and turn it all the way down.

5 | DON'T HATE THE PLAYER; HATE THE GAME

I live in a college town, so I go to church with a lot of Bible scholars and theologians. When I'm struggling with something in the Bible, I often ask these friends their opinions in the hope they can get me unstuck. It's a nice perk, having this sort of scholarly access in my church.

A few years ago, I was totally stumped by what is likely the most bizarre incident in the entire Old Testament. The passage is Exodus 4:24–26. Before the events in question, God has just commissioned Moses to go to Egypt to confront Pharaoh, demanding that he "let my people go!" So Moses goes to Egypt, taking along his wife, Zipporah, and their son. And then this happens: "On the way, at a place where they spent the night, the Lord met [Moses] and tried to kill him. But Zipporah took a flint and cut off her son's foreskin, touched his feet with it, and said, 'Truly you are a bridegroom of blood to me!' So he let him alone. It was then that she said 'a bridegroom of blood,' because of the circumcision."

Sadly, Cecil B. DeMille did not include this event in his Hollywood epic *The Ten Commandments*. I would have liked to have seen Charlton Heston try to pull off this scene. You might not know a lot about the Bible, but anyone should be able to appreciate the oddity of this story, why God would commission Moses and then unexpectedly try to kill him, to say nothing about why Zipporah's strange actions saved the day. Flummoxed by this passage and wanting to make sense of it, I approached John Willis at church. John was a legendary Old Testament Bible scholar, so I figured if anyone could help illuminate this crazy story about a hastily conducted flint knife circumcision and the "bridegroom of blood," it would be John.

"Dr. Willis," I asked John one Sunday, "what's going on with that crazy story in Exodus 4? Where God tries to kill Moses?"

John smiled and said, "I actually wrote a book about that."

I laughed and said, "Of course you did."

Over the last thirty years, psychologists have been turning their attention to what is called *positive psychology*. For most of its history, psychology had focused on mental illness and its treatment, negative and unpleasant human experiences. But a few decades ago, psychologists started asking the question, "We know a lot about mental illness and how to treat it, but what if we started focusing more on *positive* psychological experiences, things like happiness and joy?" This question gave birth to the positive psychology movement, the study of human flourishing. As an area of research, positive psychology has exploded. Courses about happiness are the largest classes on college campuses. Podcasts and books regularly share the fruits and insights from the science of human flourishing. Wherever you turn, you bump into research about how to lead a more joyful, more meaningful, and happier life.

We're going to talk about this research, the science of joy, but I want to start us off in an unexpected location. Something I expect you don't think about all that much when you try to reach for joy. Did you know that *humility* is the foundation of happiness?

Humility has been slow to arrive on the scene of positive psychology. The delay was due to measurement. A lot of the things we study in positive psychology are easily measured with self-report scales. I can ask you, for example, how happy you are or how grateful. But consider how self-report questions would try to capture humility:

Please rate the following statements from 1 = strongly disagree to 5 = strongly agree:

1. I am very humble.

2. People consider me to be very humble.

3. Humility is one of my greatest attributes.

You can see the problem! How can you rate yourself as being humble without that being, well, not very humble? To "strongly agree" that you are humble is a bit egoistical. There's something in the very nature of *self*-assessment that makes it impossible for measuring humility. That problem bedeviled humility researchers for many years, delaying humility from entering the conversations we've been having about happiness and joy. And yet the paradox that makes humility so difficult to assess with self-report is the very secret of humility's power in unleashing joy in our lives. Research has shown how humility helps us cope with life stress and trauma, from dealing with everyday relational problems to the death of a close friend. Humility also protects you from mental health issues, from anxiety to depression.

You might find the mental health benefits of humility puzzling, even paradoxical. This is why I shared with you the story of John at my church.

Most of us have a very confused vision of humility. We tend to think that humility is thinking *less* of yourself by way of self-evaluation. And if that were so, you'd be right in being puzzled about how humility sets a good foundation for mental health. Being critical of yourself isn't a recipe for happiness. So, clearly, the research is telling us that humility is something different from popular conceptions. To be sure, humility is concerned with how we stand in relation to ourselves, but humility isn't about punching holes in our egos. Humility has nothing to do with humiliation.

So what is humility? My story about John gives us a clue, and it's one you can see among your own family, friendships, and coworkers. Who are the humblest people you know? And what makes you see them as humble? The humblest people we know aren't the anxious and insecure ones, those who think less of themselves when compared with others. No, the humblest people we know are quite secure, talented, and accomplished. The critical difference is that they carry those accomplishments and skills very, very lightly. They don't brag or boast. They don't need to be the smartest or most successful person in the room. Humble people don't need to win every argument. They don't namedrop. They don't anxiously pad their résumés or feel the need to toot their own horn. Humble people are more interested in *you* than they are in *themselves*.

Simply put, humility isn't about being self-critical; it is, rather, being less invested and wrapped up in yourself. This is why egoistical and competitive people are anxious. Narcissists are compensating for felt insecurities. Humble people, by contrast, are secure in their own skin. And this comfort with themselves allows humble people to step away from social games of self-promotion and one-upmanship.

John passed away in 2023. Story after story, as we grieved and celebrated his life, revealed why I, along with so many, considered him to be one of the humblest people I knew. John was a world-renowned Bible scholar, but you'd have never known it if you sat next to him in a Bible class at church. John was never interested in being the expert in the room. He was happy to share all the stuff he knew, like crazy stories from Exodus, but he never advertised his expertise to draw attention to or elevate himself. And if that sounds healthy and well-adjusted, it is, and it illustrates how humility paves the road toward joy.

If stepping away from ourselves quiets the ego and turns down the volume of the self, humility continues this journey.

Psychologists have defined humility as a list of psychological and relational characteristics and capacities. An influential list of these capacities comes from the psychologist June Tangney. According to Tangney, humble people possess the following qualities:

- An accurate assessment of yourself
- An ability to acknowledge your mistakes and limitations

THE SHAPE OF JOY

- An openness to other viewpoints and ideas
- An ability to keep your accomplishments in perspective
- A low self-focus
- An appreciation of the value of all things, including other people

A second influential list, overlapping some with Tangney's but also different in some points, comes from the researchers Joseph Chancellor and Sonja Lyubomirsky. Humble people possess or are characterized by the following:

- A secure, self-accepting identity
- A view of yourself free from distortion
- An openness to new information, being teachable
- Being other-focused rather than self-focused
- Possessing egalitarian beliefs, that is, seeing others as having the same intrinsic value/importance as oneself; lacking feelings of superiority

These lists might be surprising. You'll notice that neither list includes "thinking less of yourself" (as in being self-critical) as a defining characteristic of humility. Humility is, rather, comprised of a mixture of *intra*personal (things having to do with myself) and *inter*personal (things having to do with others) aspects. Regarding intrapersonal traits, how I stand in relation to myself, humble people possess an *accurate*, rather than *distorted*, view of themselves. I don't falsely inflate my ego, *but neither do I disparage myself and tear myself down*. Humble people see themselves clearly. Phrased another way, *humble people accept themselves*, which creates a secure and grounded personality. This groundedness, this comfort with yourself, allows humble people to admit mistakes, listen to others, welcome difference, and accept critical feedback. Humble people aren't paralyzed by a fear of making a mistake in front of others. Humble people can, in the words of Brené Brown, "dare greatly" because they are not afraid to fail. Last, and building on what we learned about the quiet ego and our internal chatter, humble people aren't curved inward upon themselves. Humble people aren't self-focused and self-absorbed.

Regarding interpersonal and relational qualities, humble people, since they aren't looking at themselves, are able to direct their attention *outward* toward others. This allows humble people to view the people around them as valuable and important. Psychologists call humility a "social oil," a relational lubricant that reduces the frictions we experience in close relationship as fragile egos rub up against each other. Humble people, since they lack huge egos, accept feedback, show interest in the opinions of others, and get along well with others. As you can guess, the "social oil" aspect of humility has become a huge focus in management and leadership circles. Humble leaders are more effective than pompous, power-hungry narcissists. The same goes for everyone at your place of work. Humble people thrive in team settings. They are nondefensive, willing to listen, coachable, and promote other people's ideas. Secure in themselves, humble people don't need to "win."

The research on humility lets us return to our honeycomb model of the ego, the six-sided way we're using to describe what it means to turn away from yourself in search of joy. We've talked about how stepping away from the self involves turning down our ego volume. We want a quiet ego:

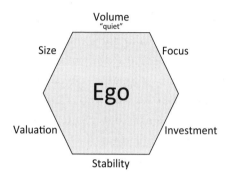

With the science of humility in hand, we can now swing around the honeycomb to describe ego *focus*, ego *investment*, ego *stability*, and ego *valuation*.

Let's start with ego focus.

Here's a confession. I'm terrible at remembering names. But the problem isn't that I don't have a good memory, or that I'm bad at remembering names. No, the reason is more depressing. When I meet people and they introduce themselves, I'm paying so much attention to myself, watching and judging how well I'm making my first impression, I simply miss what people are saying to me. I'm so self-focused when I meet people that I don't catch their names.

My problem with names is a silly and embarrassing example, but it illustrates the idea of ego focus. Where is your attention directed: inward or outward? Humble people, since they are comfortable in their own skins, are able to be more other-focused than self-focused. A simple metric of how self-focused versus other-focused you are is paying attention to how good a listener you are or how much you struggle with impatience and irritation. Self-focused people aren't very good listeners. I remember when I was in graduate school and had my very first therapy clients. I found listening to be hard and effortful. I still do. I generally give people, even my family, only a bit of my attention. Self-focused people also struggle with impatience because they constantly feel that their agenda is being frustrated by the demands of others. Other-focused people, by contrast, can more easily and quickly set their interests aside to attend to the needs of those around them. Given how their attention is directed outward, humble people are much more alert to the needs of others and quick to spot them. Other-oriented people can be present with others.

One of the reasons we become overly self-focused is because we are overly invested in our egos. By "overly invested," I mean overly *absorbed* with ourselves. Humility involves being self-forgetful, just not thinking all that much about yourself. A self-forgetting ego is called *hypo-egoic*. A famous quote sums it up well: "True humility is not thinking less of yourself; it's thinking of yourself less."

Understanding humility as hypo-egoic self-forgetfulness helps us see why humility has nothing to do with feeling bad about yourself. Being humble isn't about self-deprecation, self-abasement, or self-flagellation. With my students, I describe this distorted view of humility as the Goldilocks theory of self-esteem.

You'll recall the story of Goldilocks and the three bears. Goldilocks finds the home of Papa Bear, Mama Bear, and Baby Bear, variously trying their chairs, beds, and porridge. Everything that is for Papa and Mama Bear is too hard or soft, too hot or cold. But all of Baby Bear's stuff Goldilocks finds "just right." In the game of self-esteem, we often get stuck in a sort of Goldilocks dilemma: How much self-esteem is just right? Too much self-esteem and we're getting a big head. Too much self-esteem and we struggle with pride, egotism, vanity, superiority, and narcissism. But we also don't want too little self-esteem; otherwise, we'd lack confidence and feel insecure. So, like Goldilocks, we spend our days trying to get our self-esteem just right, not too much and not too little. We tend to think that humility is a tool in playing this Goldilocks game. When we get too prideful, we use "humility" to knock ourselves down a few pegs. "Humility" is something we do to get our self-regard lowered to the "just right" location.

Treating humility as a move in the Goldilocks game is why we send such mixed messages to our children in the face of their successes and failures. When our children fail, we pump them full of praise, trying to keep their self-esteem inflated. But when our children succeed, we withhold praise or chastise them for displays of pride. We use our praise, doling it out or withholding it, to keep a child's self-esteem in that just-right Goldilocks range. In this Goldilocks game of self-esteem, humility is the lever we feel we have to pull when we experience success. The fear is that if we don't, we'll puff up with pride. That this entire enterprise is counterproductive should come as no surprise. It's wearying and confusing to know how proud we should feel about our accomplishments without becoming an egomaniac. And it's exhausting for both parents and children to constantly manipulate a child's ego with praise or criticism. But as we're learning here, this is the wrong way to think about humility. Humility isn't about playing a Goldilocks game, trying to be humble in the face of our successes. Humility isn't about putting ourselves down. The point of humility isn't to think *less* of yourself but to *think less about yourself*.

This insight clarifies why trying to assess humility with a self-report instrument feels so wrongheaded. Self-report scales ask you to *evaluate* and *assess* yourself. This self-assessment asks you to play the Goldilocks game: How do you see yourself? Are you good or bad? Worthy or unworthy? Humble or proud? But humility, I hope you're coming to see, isn't about rating yourself *down* in a game of self-evaluation. Humility is, rather, *stepping away from self-evaluation altogether.*

This is what we mean when we describe humility as a hypo-egoic state, about self-*forgetting* rather than self-*evaluating*. And it's this self-forgetting that allows you to be other-focused. If I weren't so self-absorbed and anxiously invested in making first impressions, if I were more hypo-egoic and self-forgetting, I'd stand a better chance at being other-focused when I meet people and more likely to remember their names.

Stepping away from the Goldilocks game sounds delightful. We'd love to be less self-absorbed and more focused on the concerns of others. We crave quieter and self-forgetful egos. But how are we to acquire a self like this?

The answer is found in the descriptions of humility I shared above. Recall how I described humility as flowing from a secure and stable identity. Humble people are grounded and comfortable with themselves.

When we describe our identity as stable, we mean that our ego is nonreactive in the face of life events. Unfortunately, though, most of us have a superhero complex, playing some game of significance. Consequently, our identity is tightly connected to some metric of "winning" or "losing." Psychologists describe this as a conditional or contingent self-esteem. We feel good about ourselves if some "condition of worth" is met or fulfilled. These conditions of worth are as unique and diverse as the hero games we play. A condition of worth can be your weight, income, health, physical attractiveness, work success, social popularity, reputation, influence, and so on. Achieve the condition of worth, and you feel valuable and significant. Fail to meet the mark, and your self-image takes a hit. Tethered to these conditions of worth, the ego is constantly reacting to life events as our fortunes go up or down, a roller-coaster ride of highs and lows. This reactive ego is fragile and unstable. A secure and stable ego, by contrast, is grounded and nonreactive. A failure or setback isn't a shock to my identity or a commentary on my worth.

The secret to achieving this sort of grounded stability is the secret we've been talking about: stepping away from yourself. More specifically, you have to put some emotional distance between your identity and the conditions of worth of your superhero complex. If the game you're playing to earn a sense of significance is making your ego reactive, constantly triggered by the ups and downs of life, the solution is clear: you have to renounce the game.

This might sound cringey, but I'll say it: the research on humility is telling us to stop hating the *player* but to hate the *game*. Humility isn't about denigrating *yourself*, the player of the hero game. *Humility is giving up the hero game.* Humility is *turning away* from the conditions of worth that fragilize and destabilize your identity.

There's a famous saying in the natural sciences: nature abhors a vacuum. The same could be said about our identities. We work at the bike pump of our superhero complex to inflate our lives with meaning, value, and significance. But as we've seen, the first step toward joy is to drop the bike pump. We give up the superhero complex.

But what will fill the void of significance within you if the hero game is left behind? If you're not winning at something, won't you face a vacuum of worthiness deep within yourself?

Recall the research of Brené Brown. You'll remember that Brown discovered that shame resiliency is rooted in a fundamental conviction: knowing that you are worthy of love and belonging. The healthy ego isn't a vacuum or a hole. Joy is rooted in the durable conviction that your life has significance and value. Psychologists describe this conviction as *unconditional* self-worth, in contrast to the instability and reactivity of the conditional, contingent self-worth of the superhero complex. A newer label for this conviction, that you are worthy of love and belonging, is *mattering*. Mattering means your life matters, no matter what. Importantly, mattering isn't earned. Mattering is a given. Mattering is an *existential fact* of your existence, a value that cannot be lost or eclipsed. This unconditional value stabilizes the ego, extracting it from the successes and failures of our hero game. With mattering, you don't have to exhaust yourself at the bike pump of self-esteem, laboring to inflate your life with value and significance. You are *already* worthy.

But this raises an obvious question: Where does mattering come from? If you struggle with feeling like your life matters, this is an urgent, pressing concern. Mattering can seem like a mental magic trick. For many people, worthiness is elusive. Where does it come from?

We'll turn to this vital and profound question in part 3, where we'll explore the science of transcendence, because mattering goes to the very heart of joy. But for now, let's put a pin in this conversation to simply note that mattering, a felt sense of worthiness that is an unconditional given of your existence, stabilizes and grounds the ego, allowing us to be less reactive to the ups and downs of life. Mattering is a psychological anchor in the storms of life.

Time to stop and summarize our progress. The burgeoning psychological research on humility continues to fill out our picture of what the ego looks like when we take the first step toward joy:

Joy starts with an ego that is quiet, where the chatter of the inner voice is turned down. When our ego volume is low, we become able to forget ourselves. This allows us to become focused outwardly toward others. We're able to be present. We can do this because our identities are stable and grounded. Having turned away from our superhero complex, our egos are no longer reactive and triggered by our successes and failures. This serenity of soul is grounded in the conviction that our lives matter, that we are worthy of love and belonging. Our self-worth is secure because our value is unconditional, a durable truth about our lives, rather than something variable and contingent.

I don't know about you, but when I look at the journey we've taken, surveying the research we've gathered around the honeycomb so far, I long for the kind of inner peace we've been exploring. Because I'm not very calm. My ego is loud. My emotions churn. I get flooded by feelings of envy and insecurity. I long to shut out the critical voice in my head. I aspire to be a better listener, able to be more present with others. I'd like to remember people's names when I meet them. I dream of being more self-forgetful, less self-absorbed and wrapped up in my own agendas and projects. I'd like to be more mindful. I want to step away from the exhausting project of my superhero complex so that I could be more grounded and secure in myself. I want my ego to be less reactive, my identity less dependent on the metrics of success by which I define my worth.

Does any of that sound attractive to you? It sounds like bliss to me, a bliss pointing the way toward joy.

6 | AMAZED AT THINGS OUTSIDE OURSELVES

I fell in love with Jana before she fell in love with me. During the early days of our courtship, Jana came to visit me when I was living at home with my parents in Pennsylvania. I was taking a gap year before I started graduate school. Preparing for Jana's visit, I knew this would be a critical time in our relationship. Jana was romantically interested in me, but not wholly sold. The days we'd spend together would be my last and final chance to win her heart. Which presented the obvious challenge: How do you get someone to fall in love with you?

Pondering the dilemma, I did what thousands and thousands of couples have done before me: I took Jana to Niagara Falls.

One of the most awe-inspiring wonders of the natural world, Niagara Falls is breathtaking. Standing on the Canadian side of the river, to get the best view full view of the Horseshoe Falls, you watch over three thousand tons of water flow over the edge per second and crash downward in an explosion of foam and mist. The constant roar of the crashing tumult of water fills your chest. Mist rises hundreds of feet into the air, dancing with rainbows on sunny days. You gape in amazement and absorb a multisensory onslaught.

Going to the next level, Jana and I put on raincoats and boarded the *Maid of the Mist*, the boat that takes you into the heart of the falls, gifting you a very wet, eye level, and panoramic view of the Horseshoe Falls. It's an unforgettable experience.

Showing Jana the natural beauty of the falls wasn't my only reason for taking her on that boat ride. Niagara Falls, if you didn't know, is the self-proclaimed Honeymoon Capital of the World. As a romantic destination, people have been falling in love at the falls for generations. I figured if the magic of Niagara Falls had worked for so many others before, it might work for me.

As I write this, Jana and I have been happily married for thirty-two years. And next to our bed, on Jana's nightstand, is a very old picture of a very young-looking me wearing a blue *Maid of the Mist* raincoat at Niagara Falls.

My plan, I think, just might have worked. Thank you, Niagara Falls.

You would be forgiven if you cynically assumed that the connection between Niagara Falls and love was due to an opportunistic Chamber of Commerce seeking to capitalize on tourism. But there is more than greed going on at the banks of the Niagara River. Research is revealing to us that it's no coincidence that Niagara Falls became the Honeymoon Capital of the World. To understand this connection, let's dive into the science of awe.

Our lives are full of moments of transcendent wonder and amazement. We stare at natural wonders like Niagara Falls and exclaim, "Wow!" or "Whoa!" We might grow silent and speechless. Nature can strike us dumb with its power and grandeur. But the wonders of the natural world can also be more fleeting and delicate. Here in Texas, the bluebonnets interrupt me every spring, as does the Monarch butterfly migration every fall. We stand under starry skies, walk sandy beaches, and climb cathedral mountains. We've all been surprised by awe.

Nature isn't the only thing that prompts feelings of wonder. Psychologists have discovered that one of the most common sources of awe is witnessing acts of what psychologists describe as "moral beauty." We observe acts of heroic sacrifice and courage, and our souls are stirred. Bearing witness to love is a miraculous thing. I still get shivers recalling the wonder I felt encountering the stories of people who would become the moral heroes in my life, people like Dorothy Day, Mother Teresa of Calcutta, Gandhi, and Martin Luther King Jr.

What are these feelings of wonder?

The psychologist Dacher Keltner, a world expert in the science of awe, has defined awe as "the feeling of being in the presence of something vast that transcends your current understanding of the world." As a feeling, awe is associated with emotions of amazement, wonder, flow, bliss, ecstasy, euphoria, and joy. But crucially for our exploration concerning the shape of joy, awe is prompted by a "presence," a presence that "transcends" normal everyday experience. Borrowing from the famous primatologist Jane Goodall, Keltner describes awe as a capacity for "being amazed at things outside ourselves."

Here with awe, facing the roar of Niagara or witnessing the courage of a civil rights hero, we begin to make our final turn toward joy. Here with awe, we are, finally, *pulled out of ourselves*. Awe flips the curvature of the self. With wonder, the collapse of the modern self is reversed. No longer turned inward, awe directs our gaze outward. In the experience of awe, we begin to make what I call the *outward turn*.

I've saved our discussion about the science of awe for this moment because awe is a fascinating bridge connecting our inner life with the outer world. Wonder affects the ego and reconfigures our sense of self. Awe creates a capacity for self-transcendence, which completes our honeycomb tour of the ego and brings us to the threshold of joy. Awe has this effect by creating what psychologists call the *small self*.

Small here doesn't mean what psychologists describe as a "squashed" self, feelings of self-degradation or self-criticism to check your ego. Frankly, I think the word *small* isn't the best word choice. But the contrast implied in "small self" is with what we'd call a "big" or "inflated" ego, what we mean when we say someone has a big head. A big, inflated ego is puffed up, self-absorbed, overly sensitive, and excessively focused on themselves. That big ego is noisy. The superhero complex is out of control. Because of this, the ego occupies a large territory in self-consciousness, leaves a bigger footprint in the psyche, which pushes the needs and considerations of others to the margins. People with big egos are selfish due to their self-absorption, only concerned with their agendas and desires. When your ego gets too big, it blocks your view of the world, blinding you to the concerns of the people around you.

However, when we encounter something *bigger than ourselves*, something transcendent, the experience of awe pulls us out of our heads and away from our internal chatter. In relation to this larger reality, I adjust the "size" of myself. I recalibrate my ego in light of an encounter with a bigger, wider world. The benefits in this resizing of our egos are both emotional and social. More than inner peace is at stake. The size of our ego affects how we treat each other. Keltner describes much of what we've already described about the wandering, default state of our minds and how awe can pull us away from that noise into healthier relationships: "When our default self reigns too strongly [and] we are too focused on ourselves, anxiety, rumination, depression, and self-criticism can overtake us. An overactive default self can undermine the collaborative efforts and goodwill of our communities. Many of today's social ills arise out of an overactive default self, augmented by self-obsessed digital technologies. Awe, it seems, quiets this urgent voice of the default self."

Triggered by awe, a smaller ego is able to get out of its own way to find its place in the larger pattern of things. The small self is a felt sense of unity and oneness within a whole. We see ourselves as a piece of a much larger puzzle. And as we find our vital and proper place in the world, we come to recognize and honor the webs of reciprocity, mutuality, and dependency that connect us to each other and to the natural world. With a smaller ego, I also face my limitations and finitude, adopting a healthier perspective about what I can and cannot realistically expect of myself. My ambitions and felt responsibilities fit more comfortably within the scope of my capacities and powers. I see myself more honestly and clearly. I don't expect more of myself or less. I also refuse to stand pridefully isolated, autonomous, independent, and alone, cutting myself off from the world and others. I embrace my dependency. I admit that I need you. I also come to recognize the urgent moral demands placed on me by reality, what the natural world and fellow human beings require by way of recognition, respect, and care. For all things, we come to see, stand or fall together. We share a common life and fate.

Here is where the connection between love and Niagara Falls comes back into view. In triggering this experience of a smaller, more connected, and relational self, research has shown how awe creates feelings of love and compassion. In pulling us out of ourselves and into a relationship with the world, awe draws us closer together. Our big and noisy egos shrink in size, and a capacity for intimacy and connection is cultivated. Our hearts begin to swell. Transcendence draws us into love.

The small self allows us to complete our honeycomb tour of the self. From a psychological perspective, what does it look like to turn away from the ego? It looks like this:

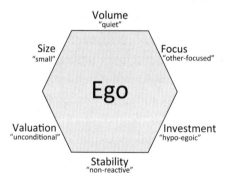

After the catastrophic collapse of the modern self—catastrophic, that is, for our mental health and relationships—I've described how our first step toward joy is a step back. We have to put some distance between ourselves and our mental chatter and the exhaustion of our superhero complex. As we've seen, what this step back looks and feels like varies depending on how you approach it. The research points to humility and toward a smaller, quieter self that is self-forgetful and more mindful, sensitive and attuned to the world around us and the needs of others. From another angle, we need a stable, nonreactive identity. When we're overly invested in the successes and failures of our superhero complex, it's hard to keep the ego quiet and small. When our value is tethered to conditions of worth, our emotions swing up and down, swaying like a boat on a stormy ocean. Consequently, stabling our inner lives demands finding a deep anchor of unconditional value and worth, the conviction psychologists call *mattering*. Of course, failures still sting. Rejections still wound. But when we matter, as waves of life crash over us, our value remains stable, grounded, and unconditional. Something very deep within us remains untouched, a place where we feel safe, tranquil, and secure.

Which brings us back to a question we left unanswered. Where can we find that safe space? In the storms of life, where are we to lower that deep anchor?

Well, if we've learned anything so far, we've learned this much: We aren't going to find this security within ourselves. The modern world has tried this path, looking for joy by turning inward. We smoked those cigarettes looking for a cure, but all we've succeeded in doing is making ourselves sicker. We need to take a different path. And our tour of the ego has pointed the way. We need to step back from ourselves.

But joy requires one additional step. Stepping *back* is a good start, but we need to take a final step *toward*.

The science of awe, along with those nagging questions about the source of our mattering, has been pointing us toward our final destination: transcendence. As we've seen in the research on wonder, transcendence cultivates a smaller, humbler self, bringing along with it all the mental health benefits we've described in our honeycomb tour of the ego. And transcendence, as we'll soon see, answers our lingering questions about the source of our ultimate value, the foundation of our significance.

It's time, then, to undertake the final stage of our journey. Awe and the small self have paved the way for us to encounter a joy found in self-transcendence, an amazement at things outside of ourselves. Here we are, at last, ready to make the outward turn.

Part 3

CURVED OUTWARD

7 | SUNLIGHT OR SHADOWS

In the early predawn hours, Beth Green was standing in front of the sink in a Bible camp bathroom. Beth was eighteen, leading Bible classes for the girl campers. The bathroom was what you'd expect for a youth camp. Mildew on the bottom of the shower curtains. The green metal doors on the toilet stalls sagged so much they couldn't lock. The floor was concrete with cracked and peeling paint.

Beth was just about to brush her teeth when her life was interrupted. A moment so overwhelming she gripped the sides of the bathroom sink. Standing there alone, in a crude camp bathroom, Beth Green encountered a reality outside of herself, something transcendent and sacred. As she described it, Beth sensed the presence of God. Her words about what transpired that morning:

> I didn't see anything. I didn't hear anything. No thunder, no heat, no light, no still, small voice. No finger writing in the steam of the mirror facing me. My toothbrush didn't levitate. The hair on my head didn't stand on end. I did not see a vision. . . . So bereft was the moment of any tangible sign, I've wished over and over to go back to the time and place and experience it again so I could

THE SHAPE OF JOY

relive it as a grown-up and put it under a theological microscope. . . .

I could have imagined it, but such things were not in my realm of thinking. I'd never heard of anyone having a remotely mystical experience. I've got no proof, of course, and really only one thing that testifies to the authenticity of it, and that's the permanence of the effects. In a lifetime of second-guesses, I've never doubted something holy and unique to my experience took place in that most unholy surrounding. Something big enough to become the before and after on my timeline.

On a lifetime roller coaster of failures and successes, losses and gains, revivals, restructures, and reversals, whatever happened that early morning has never let me go.

That eighteen-year-old Bible camp teacher would go on to become Beth Moore, one of the most popular and influential speakers and authors in the Southern Baptist denomination. Later in life, as a woman in a patriarchal religious community, Moore faced constant, and often demeaning, questions and criticism from her fellow evangelicals. Things eventually came to a head in 2016 when Moore, a survivor of sexual abuse, criticized evangelical leaders for supporting Donald Trump after the release of the *Access Hollywood* recordings. The resultant firestorm and controversy eventually led to Moore cutting ties with the Southern Baptist Convention and joining the Episcopalian church.

As Beth Moore recounts in her autobiographical memoir *All My Knotted-Up Life*, she faced multiple challenges in her life: sexual abuse at the hands of her father, the chronic mental illness of her husband, and the oppressions she experienced as a woman within the denomination she grew up in. And yet, through it all, her teenage experience in a camp bathroom, where she felt the presence of God, was and remained a stabilizing force in her life. Despite all the pain and heartbreak, the successes and the failures, Moore had made contact with a transcendent reality that anchored both her identity and calling. Gripping that sink, the eighteen-year-old Beth Moore stood amazed at something outside herself.

"Imagine some people chained deep in a cave."

This isn't a pitch for a horror movie, and I'm paraphrasing a bit, but this is how one of the most famous allegories in the world begins.

The narrator is Socrates, the ancient Greek philosopher and sage. As the voice of Plato, Socrates is sharing what is called the Allegory of the Cave from book 7 of Plato's *The Republic*. Socrates goes on, and I'll continue to paraphrase: "Imagine some people chained deep in a cave. Imagine they have been chained in that place for their entire lives. Behind them burns a fire, which they are unable to turn around and view. The fire casts a light on a blank wall before the captives, where shadows can be seen dancing. The shadows are those of puppets who are being controlled by puppeteers. The prisoners in the cave watch the shadow play on the wall before them. This shadow play, these dark figures and their voices, is the only reality the prisoners ever know."

I understand that this is a very unrealistic premise, but stay with me.

"Now imagine," continues Socrates, "that one of the prisoners is released. She stands, turns, looks around. She sees the fire, the puppets, and the puppeteers. Slowly, she comprehends the truth. Her reality was an illusion. What she thought was true was merely shadows. Eventually, she spots the opening of the cave. She follows the winding path upward and outward, to stumble, finally, into the full blaze of the sun. Having lived her whole life in darkness and firelight, the radiance of the sun blinds and disorients her. But soon her eyes adjust. For the first time in her life, she will behold the dazzling reality of the world."

I expect you've heard of the Allegory of the Cave. And even if you haven't, it's a popular trope in fantasy and science fiction, the notion that the reality you're living in isn't real but is actually an illusion. Like the Keanu Reeves character Neo in the movie *The Matrix*, you're living in a false reality and are given the chance to see the world truthfully and clearly. The red pill or the blue pill? One of them will lead you out of the cave. According to the Allegory of the Cave, the world we are currently experiencing isn't really real but shadowy, illusory, and false. We need to escape the darkness of the cave into the full light of the sun. Falsehood is exchanged for truth and shadows rejected for reality.

This journey into the sunlight makes for a good philosophical yarn or a gripping sci-fi adventure, but what do shadows and sunlight have to do with joy?

I've repeatedly said that the final step of joy involves an outward turn. The curvature of the self needs to be inverted and reversed. In the words of Augustine, instead of being *incurvatus in se*, "curved inward" on ourselves, we become *excurvatus ex se*, "curved outward." The science of awe has pointed the way. We leave the shadowy cave of the modern self, with all its chattering, anxious noise, to stand dazzled and amazed at something outside of ourselves. But if that is so, we quickly face a pressing, burning question: What lies beyond the cave? Is there a reality and truth to be found outside ourselves? What are we turning *toward* when we turn *away* from ourselves?

What is this sun that blazes outside the cave of your mind?

Pull up a chair. It's time, finally, to have a chat about transcendence.

As the science of awe has shown us, and as we'll more deeply explore, transcendence is the key to joy. Research is showing us that self-transcendence, escaping the cave of your mind to step out into the sunlight, is the path toward mental health and psychological resiliency. However, for some of us, it is difficult to have an honest and direct conversation about transcendence in our technological, scientific age. We're going to have to question and challenge some habits of mind. If we want joy, we need to overcome some modern biases and prejudices about the nature of reality. For example, Socrates goes on in the Allegory of the Cave to describe how the released prisoner returns to her enslaved companions, sharing with them the glories of the world beyond the cave. But they refuse to listen, considering her mad and insane. They choose shadows over sunlight. I fear you might have a similar reaction when we talk about transcendence. You might not believe that the sun is real.

That we're skeptical about transcendence goes back to something I shared earlier, about the inward turn made by the philosopher René Descartes. Recall, Descartes *looked for truth inside his own mind*, denying the reality of the world around him. We've inherited this radical skepticism. At the start of this cultural trend, the skepticism was mainly directed at faith, religion, and spirituality. Spiritual truths and sacred realities were denied as being "unscientific." There was no factual proof of a transcendent reality. The spiritual world, being invisible, was dismissed as fanciful and make-believe. But as we noted, the skepticism hasn't stopped there. The corrosion has continued. Today, even facts are denied as we move more deeply into a "post-truth" culture full of science denialism and fake news. We've reached the end game here. Truth is now wholly subjective, something we make up for ourselves. Reality has become a game of shadows playing out in the cave of the mind.

And so, on our journey toward joy, we face here a puzzling challenge. Can we convince ourselves that reality is real? Especially those invisible, spiritual realities our ancestors took to be manifestly obvious? Simply put, when we turn outward and speak of transcendence, is there anything out there? If you leave the cave, will you *really* see the sun?

Let me be brutally honest. Psychologists who study joy and happiness are coy on this point. They know the research, but almost every book and podcast on the market sharing the science of joy, awe, gratitude, meaning in life, mattering, happiness, and human flourishing hedges on this central question, the question of transcendence. Scientists are happy to let their research lead you to the very edge of the cave. Because the science is clear on these points: You have to exit the cave. Transcendence is the secret to joy. Faith and spirituality are good for your mental health. Study after study has shown this. Joy has a shape. The secret to happiness is turning outward. But the question nags: Is any of this invisible, spiritual stuff really real?

Following their data, the scientists of joy will point you out of the cave. But on the threshold, scientists can stop and get shy. Since science can't confirm that anything outside the cave is "real," they go mum on this point. Science knows the *direction* of joy and is happy to hand you a map, but science is silent on the *source* of joy.

You and I, though, we'll be a bit bolder. I'm going to ask that you leave your skepticism at the door of the cave. Step outside. Be amazed and dazzled by something outside yourself. I've got news for you. The sun is real.

Of course, the rebuttal here is that faith and spirituality are simply projections, like a movie camera, of our own inner lives on a mute, blank existence. There's no meaning out there in the world, only the meaning we impose on reality. Like seeing animal shapes in the clouds. Spiritual realities and truths are not really there. There is no sun, only realities and truths we wish and believe existed.

I'm sure you can see the problem here with this view of transcendence and spirituality. To put the issue plainly, if you're just projecting your inner life onto the world, you're not transcending anything. You're still trapped in the cave. That is not being awed by a reality *outside of yourself.*

If the sun isn't real, there's just the cave. Transcendence isn't transcendence if the self is still trapped in shadows. On the journey toward joy, you face, at this critical moment, a fork in the road. And sadly, the scientists won't offer you any help. The next step is all your own. Either transcendence leads you out into the sunlight, or you remain in the cave. That's your choice, sunlight or shadows.

Sunlight or shadows isn't an esoteric, mystical, or philosophical question. As I've shared, the reality of transcendence has real-world, mental health consequences. Consider the insightful 2023 essay in *The New Atlantis* written by James Mumford and entitled "Therapy beyond Good and Evil: A Nonjudgmental Psychology Is Failing Patients Who Need to Hear Hard Truths."

In his poignant and personal reflections, Mumford describes his experience battling bipolar disorder as a client in an inpatient psychiatric hospital. Mumford shares an exercise conducted by the hospital psychologist, who asks the patients to generate a list of their values. This values-clarification exercise generates a hodgepodge of answers, from hobbies to interests to virtues, from "skiing" to "honesty." The patients are then asked to circle which values resonate with them, which values on the list best capture their own values. Having identified these, Mumford recounts the sermon preached by the psychologist: "The psychologist, with a flourish, ventures an observation. Each of us, he says, has *different* values. What's more, we often *disagree* about our values. 'So,' he concludes, 'values are subjective.' And our recovery, our restoration to sanity, hinges upon our willingness to choose our own values."

Mumford, an ethics professor at the University of Virginia, recoils at this exercise. His disappointment with the psychologist goes to the question about if anything is real outside of the cave. Because if the values that guide our lives aren't solid and real, then how is a values-clarification exercise going to help us escape being trapped within ourselves? If these values are just "me" written in disguise, the self staring at itself in a mirror, I'm still chasing my own tail. I remain lost within myself, looking for answers that I do not have. As Mumford goes on to say:

> When [the psychologist] claims that "values are subjective," he is painting a picture of the world according to which the only values that exist are ones *we* have created. To say values are subjective is to say there is nothing independent of our own minds . . . [that our values] do not track a reality which is "there anyway." According to his picture, values are *determined*, not *discovered*, and selfhood—what it means to be a person—is therefore fundamentally about *choice*, not *vision*. It is about picking a course of action arbitrarily, not about seeing a reality that transcends you—goodness—and integrating with it.

"This relativism, for someone who is depressed," concludes Mumford, "doesn't alleviate the problem; it compounds it." When you're depressed, living in the cave of your mind is a nightmare.

Remember what we learned about mattering and ego stability. When we are depressed, we are haunted by a felt sense of worthlessness. In light of that self-assessment, Mumford goes on to ask the critical question: Where is my value located and secured if, in the end, all values are relative, made-up, and wholly subjective? Mumford hammers home the point: "My life doesn't feel as though it's amounted to much. So now, in my own eyes, according to my own perspective, I'm not feeling that *I* amount to much. I can't see much worth in myself or in my life. Well, if value is subjective, and I'm struggling to behold any worth in my life, who can tell me I'm wrong?"

Mumford quotes the Welsh writer Michelle Thomas, who describes depression as being "exhausted from carrying the weight of your own worthlessness." Your superhero complex has crashed and burned. In light of that heavy burden, we need to step out of the cave and into the sunlight to receive a value—a transcendent source of mattering—that exists independently of our successes and failures. Mattering isn't a subjective game of self-delusion or a therapeutic mind hack. Mattering exists *beyond* your depression. Beyond your self-talk. Psychologists describe mattering as "existential significance." Not *therapeutic* significance, E-X-I-S-T-E-N-T-I-A-L significance. Some psychologists call it *cosmic* significance. Mattering *exists*. Mattering is an *objective truth* discovered outside the cave of your mind. Your value is a *fact* that exists *beyond your self-assessment*. Your mattering is a constituent part of the cosmos, as real as gravity and groundhogs. Some values are not up for grabs. Some values are simply true. And our mental health depends on these truths. As James Mumford concludes, we need to encourage those struggling with mental health issues "to search for values *beyond* themselves."

If you count yourself a spiritual or religious person, you don't need much convincing about any of this. It's all quite obvious. Plain as the nose on your face. You know that the source of your worth is real, a fact to be recognized and a gift to be received. Brené Brown called it *grace* and named it as the antidote to shame. You might praise God here. The recovery community surrenders to their Higher Power. First Nations peoples thank the Great Spirit. The Dutch describe *ietism*, which roughly translates as "Something-ism," the conviction that there is *Something* out there in the universe that anchors our values and gives life deeper meaning. However you name it—*God*, your *Higher Power*, or just *Something*—you don't need convincing that the sun is shining.

But skeptics remain. Due to its "invisibility," the factuality of transcendence is questioned. Transcendence can feel a bit woo-woo. If you find yourself in this group, let me say a few more things to help nudge you out of the cave of your mind.

One of the reasons I shared Plato's Allegory of the Cave is because we moderns view transcendence very differently from how our ancestors once perceived it. For most of human history, it was the material, physical, and factual world—the world that we can see, smell, taste, and touch—the was fleeting, corruptible, mutable, unstable, and changing. The material world was ghostly and spectral. What our senses revealed couldn't be trusted. The physical world was the world of the cave, the realm of illusions and shadows. The transcendent, spiritual world, by contrast, was real, solid, constant, secure, permanent, and unchanging. The spiritual realm was where transcendent values were located—truth, beauty, and goodness. These values blazed steady and eternal in contrast to the fleeting shadows of the material world.

Today, we see the situation as the exact opposite. Our modern assumption is that the material, physical world is sturdy and solid. Facts disclose the truth. The stuff you can see and touch is real. By contrast, we doubt transcendence. We're skeptical about invisible things. The spiritual realm is ghostly. Unseen things are fictions. We stare at the sun—the blazing fire of the true, the beautiful, and the good—and call it a fairy tale.

Our joy depends on challenging this modern habit of mind, our kneejerk skepticism of transcendence. For generations, we've followed thinkers like Descartes and Freud inside the dark caverns of the self, searching for joy. We didn't find it. It's time to turn around and walk back out into the sunlight. But as Plato warned us, this might be a disorienting experience. So be alert to some initial blindness as you confront the factuality of invisible things. Having lived with shadows your whole life, it may take a moment to adjust to the light.

So let me help with this: What could it possibly mean to say that transcendence is real?

The realness we experience, say, in a moment of awe or in a religious experience, like the one experienced by a teenage Beth Moore in a camp bathroom is a combination of two things that on the surface seem paradoxical. The first aspect of transcendence was nicely described by William James, whom we've met already, in his book *The Varieties of Religions Experience*, the first significant scientific exploration of the psychology of transcendence. James describes our encounter with transcendence as a "reality-feeling," what could be described as an ontological intuition or an ontological emotion. *Ontology* is the word philosophers use to describe the nature of existence, what we consider to be "real." In our encounter with transcendence, we intuit, feel, or experience that Something or Someone is there, something solid and real, a Something or Someone that exists independently of and outside of my own consciousness and experience. As William James described it, in our encounter with transcendence, I experience a "sense of reality, a feeling of objective presence, a perception of what we may call 'something there,' more deep and more general than any of the special and particular 'senses' by which current psychology supposes existent realities to be originally revealed." We encounter *Something There* that is deeper and more penetrating than what mere eyesight can reveal. Deeper truths and realities. Consequently, I don't experience transcendence as a "subjective" state, as the product and projection of my own mind imposing an image on a blank canvas, like a movie projection on a screen. During an experience of awe or in a religious encounter with God, I'm not locked in the cave of my own mind. I have, rather, bumped into Something outside of myself. Or, in the case of Beth Moore, *Someone* bumps into you. Transcendence is experienced as "objective," an encounter with a Reality that exists independently of myself. And here lies the psychological power and potential of transcendence: the possibility of being *pulled out of yourself* and into a richer, deeper, fuller, and more multicolored reality. At long last, you escape the cave of your mind.

And yet the objective realities we experience in transcendence escape any material or scientific description. As a spiritual encounter with Reality, what we intuit is invisible and cannot be detected by any tool of empirical measurement. No Geiger counter will click. No lab test will come back positive. No scale will weigh it. No seismograph will wiggle. No thermometer will drop. No microscope will bring it into view. We are speaking of nonmaterial truths and realities. Consequently, as modern people who doubt invisible things, our intuitions are pulled in two directions. We are regularly amazed at things outside of our heads but wonder if, in the end, it was all just inside of our heads. As Beth Moore describes her camp bathroom experience, she admits to having "no proof" and that she "could have imagined it." But the ontological emotion, the "reality-feeling," was overwhelming.

The encounter was real, more real than anything else in her life. As Moore says, "I've never doubted something holy and unique to my experience took place in that most unholy surrounding . . . whatever happened that early morning has never let me go."

To help you see the invisible facts surrounding you, consider a scientific description of a human person. We could perform this description at different levels of analysis, from the subatomic up to the biological. Let's enter in the middle, somewhere between electrons and organs, and use the tools of organic chemistry. What chemicals make up a human? Well, over half of a person is just water. So we're composed of a lot of oxygen and hydrogen. Beyond H_2O, a human person is mostly composed of carbon, nitrogen, calcium, and phosphorus, along with a few other trace elements. Sold on the market, these chemicals would add up to about $150.

A chemical description of a human is important and valuable. Knowing you're mostly made up of water will, I hope, remind you to stay hydrated today. Lower-level physical descriptions of the human (electrons, neutrons, protons, quarks) and higher-level physical descriptions (liver, brain, lung, muscles, tendons, bones, heart, nerves, blood verses) are also legitimate and important. But we also know that something critical is being left out of each of these descriptions. Something *invisible* yet *real* has escaped scientific detection. And it's this invisible-yet-real aspect of a person—think here of someone you love—that you and I would consider to be the most real and important thing about that person. We call this invisible fact their "value" or "worth." The same value and worth you and I also possess. Something transcendent and sacred shines in humans. Shines out, really, from all of reality. And this light, if you pause to notice it, affects you.

Tugs on you. Makes demands of you. Calls to you. Nudges you. You're in a relationship with this light. You recognize it, accommodate it, nurture it, and care for it. The world is immersed in a radiant light, a shining brilliance that pulls you, if you let it, out of yourself and into life.

The sociologist Hartmut Rosa describes this relational encounter with the world as *resonance*. The world hums and vibrates with meaning. Reality speaks to us, addresses us, calls us to action, and places duties on us. A resonant encounter with life is suffused with *significance*, significances that *concern* us. These concerns pull us away from narcissistic self-absorption or depressive self-rumination. A resonant encounter with the world is to recognize a *sacred presence*. Emotions of gratitude, wonder, and love swirl here.

Also, consider this curiosity about the science of awe. It's easy to see how nature can amaze us. Nature is visible, and few would doubt the reality of Niagara Falls. But research has shown that goodness—value itself—is the most potent and powerful source of awe. More moving than nature itself and any natural wonder. A simple act of kindness is more wonderful to behold than the mighty roar of Niagara. As Dacher Keltner describes, in summarizing his cross-cultural research on awe (his italics): "What most commonly led people around the world to feel awe? Nature? Spiritual practice? Listening to music? In fact, it was *other people's courage, kindness, strength or overcoming*. Around the world, we are most likely to feel awe when moved by *moral beauty*. Exceptional physical beauty, from faces to landscapes, has long been a fascination of the arts and sciences, and moves us to feelings of infatuation, affection, and, on occasion, desire. Exceptional virtue, character and ability—moral beauty—operate according to a different aesthetic, one marked by a purity and goodness of intention and action."

The invisible world of values, the sunlight that shines forth from moral beauty, is more powerful than oceans and mountains in pulling us into amazement and wonder. Transcendent values, the *invisible facts* of the world, from the intrinsic worth of human beings to the moral values that guide righteous action, cannot be detected by any invention of science. Yet these invisible facts are the most potent force in our lives—guiding our steps, shaping our judgments, informing our choices, forming our character, nurturing our dreams, and guiding our hearts. Your life is pushed and pulled by tidal forces far more powerful than the law of gravity.

Perhaps you have had a transcendent, spiritual experience like Beth Moore. You might be a mystic, religious, or a deeply spiritual person. You might believe in God or a Higher Power. If so, you need no convincing that the sun is real. You see the world shining. You experience the wonder and awe looking into the eyes of another human being. You get chills witnessing a random act of kindness. You already know that joy has an eccentric shape, that happiness and wholeness are found in resting outside of yourself. You've already left the cave.

But some of us continue to need a bit more convincing. I wrote this chapter for you, the doubters and skeptics, those who question the invisible facts of life and have settled for shadows. You think that transcendence is a figment of your imagination. A fairy tale to help us cope with the sadness and tragedy of life.

I sympathize. I once shared those very same doubts. But if the chatter of your mind has gotten too loud, if the bike pump of your superhero complex is exhausting you, if your life has lost resonance, if the world no longer shines for you, if you are exhausted from carrying the weight of your own worthlessness, well, can I suggest that maybe it's time to get up and leave the cave? The word *transcendence* comes from Latin words meaning "to go beyond." Joy starts by going *beyond yourself*. And that includes your doubts and skepticism. It's not enough to step *back* from yourself, as helpful as that is. You have to step *outside*. The invisible facts of the world are shining around you.

Sunlight or shadows?

The choice is yours.

8 | ALL THE WAY HOME

I had been invited to speak at a business school in Michigan. The invitation was to talk, as a psychologist, about identity and mental health. As you can imagine, many business school graduates get trapped by the superhero complex of the American meritocracy. Status anxiety drives these students toward visions of financial and corporate success. They have to climb, achieve, and win. Even before graduation, every classmate is a potential competitor—for grades, coveted internships, and graduate schools. After graduation, these gladiators of capitalism will fight over jobs, salaries, promotions, and advancement.

The label *neoliberalism* is often used to describe the American success ethos. Neoliberalism concerns how the competitive logic of markets has infiltrated almost every aspect of American life. Families compete to get their children into elite preschools, then grade schools, then high schools, then colleges, then graduate schools, and then, finally, we enter the arena of the corporate world. We've been competing our entire lives. Our life is the Game of Thrones. Every human interaction is reduced to comparison and competition. In this neoliberal world, friends are mostly frenemies, potential rivals whose success can make us feel anxious and insecure.

That was my audience at the business school. I was invited to speak about the status anxieties of the students, to offer medicine for the psychological and relational harms being done by the neoliberal superhero complex. I shared the message about identity I've shared with you: Your mattering, your value and identity, cannot be attached to metrics of winning or losing. Otherwise, your mental health will be a yo-yo, up and down, alternating between shame and success. And given that neoliberal competition is a contest of king of the hill, 99.99 percent of us are going to fail to summit the mountain of our dreams. Even the winners will have to perpetually watch their backs. It's the law of the jungle. Someone is always gunning for you.

"The science tells us," I shared with my business school audience, "that psychological resilience flows out of mattering, what psychologists call existential or cosmic significance. The durable conviction that you matter, no matter what." I hope I've also convinced you of that. Your value can't be the football in a neoliberal game of competition. Your worth cannot be a prize that you can win or lose.

When I got home from the talk, Jana asked me, "How'd it go?"

"Well," I responded, "I got them to third base, but I think some of them were stranded. I couldn't bring them all the way home."

Here's what I meant. It's easy to tell people they matter, to insist that they need to recognize a transcendent truth about themselves. But if you don't believe that the sun is real, if you don't step out of the cave, if you deny transcendence, you're pretty much stuck. If mattering is a value that exists independently of your self-assessment, an invisible cosmic fact, and you deny that such values are real, well—*poof!*—mattering evaporates. All you are left with is the superhero complex, and your happiness becomes a game of yo-yo. Up and down, up and down.

So you can appreciate the problem I faced at the business school. I could speak about the science of mattering. I could take those anxious students to the edge of the cave. I could get their joy to third base. But to bring them all the way home, I had to talk about transcendence. I had to speak of the reality of indivisible facts. But in secular business schools, talk about transcendence and spirituality can make you sound soft-headed. So I stuck to the science: mattering is predictive of mental health. *How* you matter, well, I'll leave that up to you.

Actually, I didn't quite leave it there. I wanted to get those stressed-out and competitive business students all the way home. In the science of mattering, psychologists make a contrast between *relational* mattering and *existential* mattering. Mattering to others and transcendent mattering. I shared that with the business students: "Where does your mattering come from? The durable conviction that your life is significant and valued, even in the midst of failure? For those of you who come from religious or spiritual traditions, you have some answers to those questions. But if you don't come from a spiritual tradition, here's the best advice I can give you: Surround yourself with people who tell you that you matter—and unconditionally so. Find people who, when life gets hard, remind you of your value and worth. Listen to the people who speak life into you."

Basically, if you don't believe—or can't believe—that you *cosmically* and *existentially* matter, you can find ways to *socially* and *relationally* matter. You can matter to someone. And be reminded by them that you matter.

Social mattering is vital for mental health, and it is a good proxy for cosmic mattering. We all know the value of family and friends in making a happy life and getting through dark times. But at the end of the day, the research has shown that cosmic mattering is the more powerful force in predicting meaning in life, which is the foundation of mental health and well-being. And if you reflect on this, it's not hard to see why. Social mattering can still leave you stranded on third base.

In 2023, the US surgeon general sounded the alarm on a rising health risk facing Americans. This new health risk is as deadly as smoking fifteen cigarettes a day. According to the surgeon general, this threat is associated with "a greater risk of cardiovascular disease, dementia, stroke, depression, anxiety, and premature death." What could be so bad for you that it is the equivalent of being a pack-a-day smoker?

Loneliness.

This might surprise you, but loneliness is a killer. The lethality of loneliness isn't just related to mental illness, to increased vulnerability to anxiety, depression, self-harm, and suicide. Social alienation and disconnection also have deleterious physical effects associated with premature mortality due to heart disease, high blood pressure, stroke, diabetes, dementia, and infectious diseases. In addition to being more lethal than smoking a pack of cigarettes a day, loneliness poses a greater health risk than drinking six alcoholic drinks per day, physical inactivity, and obesity.

These statistics are alarming given how loneliness has reached epidemic proportions. As the Surgeon General Advisory shares, one out of every two Americans report experiencing loneliness, with the highest rates found among young adults. Young people report greater periods of social isolation (days without any social contact) and fewer and fewer close friendships. Membership in local churches and faith communities has been steadily declining and community involvement evaporating. And then there's the biggest paradox: Social media makes it all so much worse. Instead of connecting us, social media keeps us alone and isolated. As the advisory summarizes one important study, "Participants who reported using social media for more than two hours a day had about double the odds of reporting increased perceptions of social isolation compared to those who used social media for less than 30 minutes per day."

The point to be observed here should be both clear and alarming. Yes, I was able to point those business school students toward social sources of mattering. But friendships are increasingly in short supply. Social mattering is a scarce resource. Fewer and fewer of us have access to it. That is the grim reality more and more of us are facing: when you're alone, there's no one to bring you home.

Do you remember when your heart was first broken?

My first love was Mary, and she broke my heart in the seventh grade. To be honest, this romance lasted only forty-eight hours. I had a crush on Mary for months, head over heels since the first day of school. I finally screwed up the courage to ask her out the way we did it back then: I passed a note to Mary's friend, asking her to deliver it. My note got right to the point: "Will you go out with me?"

Very romantic.

Soon, Mary's friend returned with her answer: "Yes."

I was over the moon. I went over to speak to her. "Hi," I said. "Hi," she said. And then I went off to hang out with my friends. The next day at school, I don't think we spoke. In the hazy fog of my memory, I can't tell if I was too embarrassed to talk to her or if that was just the way we dated back then. "Dating," as best as I can recall, was a theoretical concept. Notes were passed and offers accepted, and that pretty much defined the relationship. New boyfriends and girlfriends didn't talk or associate any more or less than they usually did. But it's not out of the realm of possibility that Mary expected a bit more attention from her new "boyfriend."

Regardless, a day later, Mary's friend delivered me a note: "I am breaking up with you." My heart cracked.

Hearts do. They crack. We are rejected, hurt, betrayed, and wounded. We can suffer abuse. We carry the scars. As I learned at an early age, falling in love is a risky and dangerous thing.

The concerns here aren't just romantic. Our families of origin are hazardous as well. The love we experience within our homes can be absent, inadequate, manipulative, or abusive. Family can mess us up in ways not easily fixed.

For my part, I've been lucky in love. But not everyone is. The problem with social mattering isn't just that love is scarce, that loneliness has become an epidemic. Love itself can be the problem. The most important people in our lives can let us down, betray and hurt us. In light of this, our mattering has to dwell somewhere beyond our saddest and most tragic love stories. As I shared with my son's graduating class, we need mattering on our *worst* days. You need to matter the day your heart is broken.

As the chair of our academic department at my university, I spend a lot of time advising my students about vocation and career choices. Years ago, I had a student who was in our premed track. She had dreams of becoming a doctor. Consequently, during her freshman year, she was enrolled in all the science and math classes the premed program requires as foundational. Advanced calculus. Organic chemistry. Introductory physics. The trouble was, while a hard worker, my student wasn't very good at math or science. This came to light after a year's worth of poor grades. In our advising meeting, I asked her if she still wanted to remain in the premed program. Yes, she replied, her dream was to become a doctor. I encouraged a pause for some career exploration, but she re-enrolled in all the math and science classes she had just failed, hoping to improve her grades. Sadly, it didn't work.

Sitting with this student after a second year of struggling, I revisited the questions from the year before: Do you still want to be a doctor? Do you want to explore other careers? Two years of poor grades, I felt, were telling a pretty obvious story. The happy news was that she had other skills, talents, aptitudes, and interests where she was experiencing success. So why not move your major and career plans in those directions, toward those strengths? Why keep banging your head against this particular wall?

It was time for me to dig a little deeper about where this dream of becoming a doctor was coming from and why my student was clinging to it so obsessively to her own detriment and harm. The answer soon emerged. She came from a family of doctors, a legacy of doctors. My student wanted to become a doctor because her *family* wanted her to become a doctor. She was trying to continue the family tradition. My student had internalized the superhero complex of her family so much that it became her complex as well. These self-inflicted wounds were being caused by a distorted self-image that originated in her family of origin.

Love is scarce. And love hurts. Love can also twist us into pretzels, distorting how we see ourselves. The famous and pioneering psychologist Carl Rogers powerfully described how this happens. According to Rogers, we all desire "positive regard." We all want to matter in the eyes of others. We crave esteem, admiration, and respect. We long for love. So *we seek our worth in the eyes of others.* A parent. A coach. A teacher. A lover. A friend. A boss. A social media audience. But the trouble with this, continues Rogers, is that people attach "conditions of worth" to their esteem and attention. Love comes with strings attached. There is a game you have to play. An appearance you must maintain. A show you are required to perform. Growing up, you absorb the conditions of worth of your family, what would win the praise and attention of your parents. Just like my student did in her family of doctors. You also navigate the conditions of worth in every friend group you've ever been a part of—discerning what was cool, what made you popular, what got laughs. And then there are the conditions of worth from our romantic and sexual histories, the way we've changed ourselves to please a partner, lover, or spouse. These are games we are still playing with family, friends, and lovers. We've adjusted ourselves to win attention and praise from teachers, mentors, and coaches. From every boss and workplace. For our entire lives, we've worked to win prizes of affection, admiration, and attention.

But the trouble brewing here is that conditions of worth distort the ego. Conditions of worth twist our self-perceptions. We spend so much time trying to please others that we lose track of ourselves. Love comes with so many strings attached we become emotional puppets chasing affirmation and affection. Positive regard is a drug. Attention is intoxicating. And like addicts, we'll engage in soul-damaging behaviors just to get a hit. We'll deny and hide truths about ourselves—shoving ourselves into a closet—to become the person others want us to be. We'll pretend. Put on a face. And over time, that pretending will take a toll. You will pay an emotional price. Pretense becomes our truth, and we end up wondering why we're so lost and unhappy. We're a round peg but have lived our lives jamming ourselves into the square holes of other people's expectations. This is the sad story that shows up over and over again in therapy. "What do *you* want?" the therapist asks. And our response is befuddlement and confusion: "I've spent my whole life trying to please other people. My family. My friends. My spouse. Truthfully, I don't know what I want. I don't think I've ever known."

According to Carl Rogers, the only way we can untie these knots is to find a place of *unconditional* positive regard, a mattering that comes with no strings attached. Zero conditions of worth. In that space, where your worthiness is held inviolate, you find room to discover yourself. You can heal. You can slowly disentangle your value from the gaze of the world.

But if that's the good news, here's the bad: Finding unconditional positive regard in another person is practically impossible. Not because our parents, friends, or spouses are cruel and mean. Just the simple truth that our parents, friends, and spouses are themselves lost and unwell. We've all been twisted and confused by our histories with conditions of worth. Our parents are damaged people. So are our friends. So are you. We come to each other with flaws, needs, addictions, compulsions, wounds, and scars. We are not perfect lovers. No one is. So we pass the damage around. And even in our most intimate relationships, we continue to hide from each other. We might feel loved unconditionally, but we are continually haunted by the fear that we can push love past the breaking point. And we never know where that line might be, where our failure might be one failure too much.

You might think that therapy provides us a space for unconditional positive regard. That was Carl Rogers's hope. And it is true that we open ourselves up to therapists in ways we struggle to do with our loved ones. We can confess secrets to therapists because therapists don't have to forgive us. Therapists aren't the ones we've harmed, betrayed, lied to, hid from, or failed. Our disclosures to our therapists come risk-free. And that's a lifesaving blessing, that space of transparency and honesty. But precisely because of these lowered emotional stakes, therapy can only provide a simulacrum of unconditional positive regard. That our therapist *isn't* a loved one is the key reason we can expose ourselves, like how we'll spill our sorrows to a bartender or hairdresser. Plus, there's the nagging fact that we have to pay our therapists to listen to us. The compassionate ear of my therapist comes with a price tag. To be clear, I'm not suggesting that therapists don't care about their clients. They do. And there is power in working through the tangles of life in an objective, warm, nonjudgmental space. But we shouldn't mistake *therapy* for *love*.

Social mattering is life-giving, but social mattering is scarce, fragile, and can twist you into knots. In the end, social mattering, for many of us, will never be able to fully provide an unconditional foundation of value, one that is wholly stable and transcendently dependable. This is not to discount the power of love. Far from it. If our epidemic of loneliness teaches us anything, it is that love is a lifeline, and without it, we drown. Facing the limitations of social mattering is, rather, simply owning the truth that love can be hard to find, that love is risky and comes with strings attached. We can find ourselves cut off from love, isolated and alone. We can be hurt by those we love. And we can lose ourselves in the eyes of others, playing games and pretending in order to win their attention and affection. When you embed yourself, as a broken and needy person, in a web of relationships comprised of other broken and needy people, you necessarily place your mental health at significant risk. As deeply flawed people, we are not infallible caretakers of each other's hearts. We can leave each other stranded on third base in our journey toward joy.

And so we come back to transcendence, to a mattering that is cosmic and existential. Again, as the research points out, cosmic mattering is more critical than social mattering. For the simple reason that you need a source of mattering on the day your heart breaks. Joy demands something that can ground and steady us in the storms of relational drama and trauma. When love hurts, we need a place to rest beyond the vagaries and inconstancies of human care and affection. We need a home when we have no home, a love that remains when lovers have forsaken us.

So let me, then, nuance the geometric metaphor we have been using. In describing transcendence as a reality "beyond" ourselves, I have described this "beyondness" as an outward turn, reversing the curvature of the self. But our experience of cosmic mattering is often felt as something deep within ourselves. Like roots searching downward for water, we make contact with the Source of our being. There we feel anchored. Grounded. We make contact with something stable, constant, and solid. The origin of this groundedness, this cosmic anchoring, is beyond and outside ourselves. We aren't performing a therapeutic trick of self-affirmation deep within our psyche. Making contact with the Reality beneath my reality isn't a self-generated illusion. You are, at the deepest levels, encountering that Something, that Power, that Love that exists independently of yourself. I may disappear, but this Something remains. I may turn away, but *It* continues to hold and carry me. Words start to fail us here, but my own experience of this encounter is similar to how the novelist Francis Spufford describes it. Spufford finds himself sitting in the pews of a quiet church. He closes his eyes and practices mindfulness. He attends to his breathing. He pays close attention to his body and the sounds in the space. His mind quiets and the ego volume is turned down. All this takes some time. But then, beyond mere relaxation, Spufford's mind is drawn more deeply into contemplation, toward a hard-to-describe encounter with the Source of our very being. Spufford writes:

> Beyond, behind, beneath all solid things there seems to be a solidity. Behind, beneath, beyond all changes, all wheeling and whirring processes, all flows, there seems to be flow itself. . . . It seems to shine, this universal backing to things. . . . It feels as if everything is backed with light. . . . And that includes me. . . . It's not impersonal. Someone, not something, is here. . . . I feel what I feel

ALL THE WAY HOME

when there's someone beside me. I am being looked at. I am being known; known in some wholly accurate and complete way that is only possible when the point of view is not another local self in the world but glows in the whole medium in which I live and move. . . .

It never stops shining. It is continuous, this attention it pays. I cannot make it turn away. But I can turn away from it, easily; all I have to do is to stop listening to the gentle, unendingly patient call it stitches through the fabric of everything there is.

When one turns *inward* to make contact with this Reality *beyond* oneself, the experience is one of stability, security, and peace. A cosmic sense of mattering is communicated, shared, and gifted to us. Thus anchored, we are equipped and protected to enter into the unpredictable world of human neediness and vulnerability. We step into relationships centered and grounded, our worth secured beyond the opinions and attention of others. Hurt, abuse, loss, and betrayal remain painful, but they do not— not ultimately or finally—penetrate to the deep Source of our mattering. In that space, held safe, I can never be unsettled. My identity shines in a continuous light. This is the deep stability that is gifted to us by a cosmic source of mattering. This is the secret behind the science, why transcendence is associated with joy.

This is how you make it all the way home.

9 | RABBIT OR DUCK?

For over ten years, I have been serving as a volunteer chaplain at a maximum-security prison here in the state of Texas. I lead a weekly Bible study and provide pastoral and emotional support for the men who attend. In caring for these incarcerated souls, many of whom I've known for years, the most anxious time for me comes during the semiannual lockdowns. During these few weeks, the religious and educational programming of the unit is halted. The men are kept locked in their cells 24/7 as security checks are made, cell by cell, throughout the entire unit. Meals are taken directly to the cells in Johnny sacks, a brown bag delivering cold sandwiches for breakfast, lunch, and dinner. Unable to leave their cells during these weeks, the men experience hunger, boredom, and a rising tide of claustrophobia. As you can imagine, lockdowns are stressful and unpleasant. And unbearably hot during the summer months. During these weeks of separation from the men out at the unit, I worry about and pray for them constantly.

After the lockdown ends and we're allowed back at the unit, I start our reunion off by checking on their emotional health, asking how they fared during their weeks locked in their cells. "How was your lockdown? How are you doing? Are you okay?"

The answers are predictable. "It was awful." "I never want to see another baloney sandwich for the rest of my life." "I was going crazy." One year, though, I was interrupted by a surprising answer from Mr. Kenneth. Kenneth is a Black man in his sixties, so out of Southern respect and habit, I call him *Mr.* Kenneth. When I asked Mr. Kenneth about his lockdown, he became rapturous. "I *loved* my lockdown! I always love my lockdown." This wasn't the answer I had expected. How could someone love something so horrible and miserable? Curious and surprised, I asked, "Really? Everyone hates lockdown, Mr. Kenneth. Why do you love it?" Mr. Kenneth smiled a beatific smile, "I love my lockdown because that's my quiet time with Jesus. There are no disruptions, no officers or knuckleheads talking to you or messing with you. There's no schedule. Nowhere you have to go. So I have all this time by myself to be with Jesus. That's why I look forward to my lockdowns."

I shook my head in amazement. If you want exhibit A for the shape of joy, look no further than Mr. Kenneth.

Joy. Awe. Gratitude. Love. Psychologists have described these experiences as "self-transcendent emotions." As you can tell by the label, these emotions involve going beyond—transcending—yourself. This is the transformative power of the outward turn. Leaving the cave to reverse the curvature of your soul. We've seen this dynamic in both the science of mattering and awe, being amazed at things outside ourselves and securing our value in cosmic, existential mattering. Now it is time to talk about joy.

Let me start by saying this: Joy is a puzzle. Joy can be hard to wrap your head around. Even the psychologists who study joy disagree about its proper definition.

On the one hand, we could think of joy as *a positive emotional state*, akin to happiness and pleasure. Understood as a positive emotion, as a synonym for happiness, lots of things in life give us joy. Good news. Success. A lovely vacation. An engrossing hobby. And yet there's a problem with defining joy as a positive emotion. Mr. Kenneth is a good example of why.

Emotions, as defined by psychologists, are triggered by external events. Something happens, and this elicits an emotional response. Witnessing an injustice makes you angry. Experiencing a loss makes you sad. In facing an uncertain future, you worry. Stimulus—response. Event—emotion. Basically, emotions are a feedback system communicating important information about what's going on in your life. Joy, in this view, is letting us know we're doing something pleasurable or that something good has happened that aligns with our life goals. As positive emotional reinforcement, joy keeps us coming back to these experiences and pursuits. Joy points us toward and brings us back to the life we want and desire.

That's all well and good until you find yourself locked in a small, hot prison cell for weeks on end eating baloney sandwiches three times a day. Where was Mr. Kenneth's joy coming from? Clearly, his joy wasn't coming from his surroundings. Mr. Kenneth's rapture wasn't being triggered by events in a stimulus-response sequence. Something else was going on. Rather than being *triggered by* events, Mr. Kenneth's joy *transcended* events. That contrast—triggered versus transcending—is the secret of joy. There is a joy that goes beyond being a mere "positive emotion," a joy that goes deeper than mere pleasure. This is the fundamental contrast between joy and happiness. *Happiness* is dictated by what *happens* to us and is therefore contingent and provisional. The words *happiness* and *happens* come from the Old Norse word *hap*, meaning "chance" or "luck." And with chance and luck, we're back to the ups and downs of a yo-yo.

In short, we need to make a contrast between joy as a *positive* emotion, as happiness or pleasure, and joy as a *transcendent* emotion, as an emotional response toward life that is *untethered* to events and environments. Such joy, like Mr. Kenneth's, does bring happiness and pleasure, but its *source* comes from *beyond* present circumstances. Such joy is immune to the yo-yo of happenstance.

There is also a moral aspect to joy. Consider how, during the Holocaust, the Nazis took pleasure in persecuting and exterminating the Jewish people. This evil made the Nazis "happy." Consequently, a person might be tempted to say the Nazis took "joy" in killing. But most of us would recoil in horror at that idea. There is a halo of goodness around joy we want to protect and preserve. Joy and evil cannot be partners. Beyond mere pleasure and happiness, we want joy to be sacred and holy, reserved for those moments when we come into alignment with something true, and beautiful, and good. We detect blasphemy at work if you say hurting people brings you "joy," a defilement of something wholesome and pure. Joy isn't found in the darkness. Joy is turning your face toward the light.

Joy, then, is more than a positive emotion. Joy isn't triggered. Joy transcends. This makes joy stable and constant when the events of our lives go up and down. Just like cosmic mattering, joy isn't conditional or provisional, attached to the environment and events. That was the secret to Mr. Kenneth's joy during his lockdowns.

Mr. Kenneth's joy is an inspiring story, but it can be hard to connect the psychological dots here. How, exactly, can we transition joy from being a *positive* emotion to being a *transcendent* emotion? How do we make the shift from triggered to transcending?

In his influential work on emotions, the philosopher Robert Roberts has argued that joy is what he calls "a concern-based construal." That's a mouthful, so let me unpack.

To start, joy is a construal. By that, we mean that joy isn't really a feeling but is, rather, a perceptual take on reality. Roberts uses, as an illustration here, this famous optical illusion:

Do you seek a duck or a rabbit? The image has two takes. We can see either a duck or a rabbit. But not both at the same time, though we can go back and forth.

Joy, says Roberts, is like the duck or rabbit illusion. Things happen to us, and we construe those events in different sorts of ways. For example, most of the men in the prison construe lockdown as a duck, as wholly miserable. That's their take, their perception of the situation. Mr. Kenneth, by contrast, sees a rabbit. Mr. Kenneth has a very different take on lockdowns, a very different way of seeing things. Understood this way, joy is less a *feeling* than a *perception*. Joy is a way of *seeing* the world.

Staying with Roberts, these construals are concern based. That is to say, our *perception* is affected by what we *care* about, the things that deeply concern us. This should be an obvious and simple point. If I don't care about something, it doesn't elicit much emotion in me. But if I care, I'll have lots of feelings.

More fully, then, joy is a way of *seeing the world through what you care about*. And here we find the answer about how we can transition joy from *positive* emotion to *transcendent* emotion. As a transcendent emotion, joy locates our cares and concerns in transcendent goods and the bliss and peace we receive in seeking and aligning with those goods. That's what Mr. Kenneth had accomplished. He didn't care about confinement or baloney sandwiches. About those things, he was *unconcerned*. Mr. Kenneth had extracted his concerns from his material fortunes and relocated them in a transcendent good. When that happens, joy, as a transcendent emotion, is no longer triggered by negative life events or relational storms. As an emotionally stabilizing force, joy confers psychological resiliency as we step into difficult and painful experiences. I'm steadier on my psychological feet because, at a deep level, my emotional responses are not 100 percent *reactive* to life. I'm no longer an emotional puppet triggered by events. Because of joy, I possess myself; I gain *emotional independence*. To be sure, I will have lots of emotional reactions to life. I will feel the waves of anger, shock, grief, rage, and sorrow crash over me. But having an emotional anchor, possessing a deep inner stability, I can keep my footing in the face of emotional tsunamis. I've been set free, psychologically emancipated and liberated. Nothing that happens to me can dictate or determine my responses. I feel self-possessed precisely because I don't, in fact, possess myself. My concerns are located *beyond* myself. I have made the outward turn. Embracing joy, I have achieved self-transcendence.

According to psychological research, meaning in life is composed of three ingredients: coherence, purpose, and mattering. Of these three ingredients, as we've discussed, mattering is the most important. But coherence and purpose are also vital, critical in helping us see rabbits rather than ducks.

If mattering points to our cosmic, existential significance, value, and worth, coherence and purpose point to the story we are telling about our lives. If joy is a concern-based construal, seeing the world through what we care about, our stories embody those values, cares, and concerns. By *coherence*, psychologists mean that our lives make sense to us. We get the plot of our life. *Purpose* describes the direction or goal of our lives, where we think our lives are going. Our story is heading somewhere. Given our deep need for coherence and purpose, our identities are *narrative* in nature. We are story-making creatures, and the story I tell about myself defines who I am. Of course, this story is constantly being revised and edited. We're continuously writing and rewriting our story to make sense of our lives. Sometimes this is easy, but sometimes this is difficult. One of the biggest reasons people seek out therapy is that they've lost the plotline of their lives. Our stories can get stuck in the mud, derailed, or reach a dead end. When this happens, when we experience narrative disruption, a lot of symptoms emerge. We feel depressed and anxious. And while we can focus on alleviating those emotional symptoms, the heart of our problem is *narrative* in nature. Healing requires telling a better story about myself. Given what has happened to me, *what new story* do I need to tell about my life? Finding this new story is how you make your way back into the light.

The big implication here is that joy depends on the story you are telling. Will your story cause you to see ducks or allow you to see rabbits? Our stories capture our concerns, and those concerns dictate how we see the world. For joy to become a *transcendent* emotion, our *concerns* must be found *beyond* ourselves, and our stories create this possibility.

In describing these stories, the psychologist Pamela King has studied what she calls a *transcendent narrative identity*. When the story of our lives is intentionally attached to sacred and transcendent values, goods, and purposes, our identities become so located, grounded, and secured. Captured and held by this transcendent story, our cares are found beyond ourselves, in all that is true and beautiful and good. We acquire the psychological capacity to construe life from a transcendent vantage point. A capacity for joy beyond mere happiness is created. Your story—how you make sense of your life, where you think your life is going, and the anchor of your cosmic value—now stands free of fickle fortune. You're telling a story now that can save you. Even on the worst day of your life. Just like Mr. Kenneth, where others see ducks, you can now see rabbits.

I was raised in a middle-class family where we had to be conscious of our budget. It was a value of my father to pay off our cars and drive them until they fell apart. Any month without a car payment was a good month. You drive your car to the breaking point.

This meant we drove some pretty sketchy cars. The most memorable one was a Buick with a green vinyl top. The sun had cracked that vinyl and turned it into a dayglo lime-green fluorescent hue. Looking at the car hurt your eyes. Beyond ugliness, the back doors didn't work due to some very significant dents, so you had to crawl over the front seat if you were a passenger. Or enter through the back windows like a NASCAR driver. Finally, the car couldn't reach its top gears and made a loud knocking noise as it reached its top speed of 45 mph.

The car was destined for the junkyard, but Dad approached the family and posited that if we would drive it for just two more months over the summer, it would be financially good for the family. All we needed during the summer was to get back and forth from Mom's place of work at the YMCA about two miles away, where we kids also had summer jobs and hung out with friends. No problem, we told my dad. We didn't mind the car. We thought it was hilarious.

My mom was in charge of the women's physical programming at the YMCA, and a few weeks into the summer, a woman in one of her fitness classes asked if she could speak privately with her. As the woman settled into a chair in my mom's office, she started her story off in a peculiar way. "Paula, do you know that green car your family drives?" My mom was mortified and started apologizing profusely. The woman was wealthy, so my mom could only imagine that, as a client of the YMCA, she was appalled by the piece of junk parked next to her Mercedes. But the woman quickly cut my mother off. "You don't need to apologize," she said. She continued, "Today, when my son and I arrived, we pulled up behind your children and your green car. After they parked, some of them climbed over the seats and out the windows." My mom again tried to apologize, but the woman held up her hand. "Watching your kids get out of the car, my son made a disparaging remark about them. Of course, only I heard him, but I wanted to come and apologize. I have failed my son as a parent. You know we have a lot of money. My son has everything he needs. But he's very selfish and entitled. When I saw your children with their friends climbing out of your car, they were all laughing and having a great time. The car didn't bother them at all. They didn't care. My son would never ride in a car like that. And in that moment, I couldn't help but make a comparison between how you raised your children and how I raised my son. Your children don't seem to care about material things, but there they were, happy and laughing with their friends. My son, as rich as we are, is sad and lonely. And for that, I blame myself."

Families also have narrative identities. And this story is a part of mine. Families repeat and share stories over and over, sharing the lore that defines who they are, what they value, and what they care about. Just like our own personal narratives, our family stories can get trapped by the superhero complex of conditional mattering. Recall my student who came from a family of doctors, how her value became attached to her ability to be good at science and math. I think of that woman from the YMCA and her son. But just like Mr. Kenneth, families can also tell a *transcendent narrative* about themselves, a bigger story about what really matters in life. In my family, the story of our green car became a part of our shared identity. Whenever we retold the story about that junky green car, we did so to laugh over memories of climbing out of its windows that summer. But something deeper was also at stake in our sharing that story over and over again. The summer of the green Buick was a parable about the shape of joy. "Joy is not found in material things," we would say to each other. "Joy is found in gratitude and love."

Gratitude is also a self-transcendent emotion. As the happy and positive emotion we feel when we receive a gift, favor, or benefit, gratitude is an *outward-facing* emotion, a thankfulness directed toward both the gift and the giver. Because of this outward-facing posture, gratitude and joy are tightly linked. Research has shown that gratitude and joy create a positive, reinforcing feedback loop, an "upward spiral" of well-being. Grateful people experience more joy. And joyful people experience more gratitude. The two emotions carry you up and up and up.

That Mr. Kenneth was both *grateful* and *joyful* for his lockdown brings us back to ducks and rabbits. Like joy, gratitude can be a mere positive emotion or a fully transcendent emotion. Because Mr. Kenneth construed his lockdown from a transcendent perspective, what others experienced as *hardship*, he experienced as a *gift*. As transcendent emotions, gratitude and joy are experiences of feeling blessed in a way that goes beyond mere happiness. Our family experience with our broken-down car illustrates the point. Objectively speaking, the car was horrible and should have triggered in us feelings of dissatisfaction and embarrassment. The exact feelings of disgust the young man directed at us in the YMCA parking lot. But we felt grateful for the car, blessed to have it. That's the psychological magic of gratitude. Junk becomes a gift. Curse becomes a blessing. Unhappiness turns to joy. The psychological power of gratitude in transforming your entire outlook on life is the reason why study after study has shown gratitude to be one of the biggest predictors of psychological well-being.

This dynamic at work in gratitude, as a transcendent emotion, is the same dynamic we've observed with both cosmic mattering and joy. When gratitude is anchored in transcendent values and goods, it becomes immune to the ups and downs of life. Notice how, with both Mr. Kenneth's lockdown and our old Buick, the material conditions remain unchanged across perspectives. Lockdowns remain lockdowns, and you still have to climb out of the windows of the car. But some people see ducks, while others see rabbits. Same material situation, two very different emotional reactions. Some people live with chronic frustration and dissatisfaction, while others feel thankful and blessed. Some spiral down, while others spiral up.

Awe. Mattering. Joy. Gratitude. Here is your roadmap to happiness. And the journey has a single destination: transcendence. Joy has a shape. The same shape as wonder, worthiness, and thankfulness. And don't just take my word for it; this is the story the science is telling. Psychological stability and contentment aren't discovered by looking inward. Happiness, peace, wholeness, and resiliency are found in connecting your story to something bigger than yourself. Study after study has shown this. In experiences of wonder and awe, transcendence creates a small self, a self that has turned away from its internal chatter to connect with a larger reality. The invisible fact of your cosmic mattering secures your value and worth in the face of loss and failure. Your mattering stabilizes your ego and creates psychological resiliency. Finally, as transcendent emotions, joy and gratitude create an upward emotional spiral, enabling you to look beyond material circumstances, in a prison or driving an old car, to experience life as graced and blessed.

This is the shape of joy. The transformative power of living *beyond* yourself.

Stop and ask yourself: Is the story you're telling about your life bringing you more gratitude and joy? Or is the story you're telling making you more fragile, triggered, and vulnerable? You are either spiraling upward or downward. It all depends on how you construe the world.

Rabbit or duck?

Take a look at your life and tell me what you see.

10 | THE LAW OF THE GIFT

A few hours before her beheading, Sophie wrote a single word on the back of the criminal indictment handed to her by the Nazis.

Sophie had been arrested four days earlier, along with her brother, Hans, caught by a janitor for secretly distributing subversive leaflets at the University of Munich. The Scholl siblings were a part of the Nazi resistance group that had named itself the White Rose. The members of the White Rose, mostly young people like the Scholls, clandestinely printed and distributed leaflets in an attempt to challenge the evils being perpetrated by Hitler and to rouse the moral conscience of the German nation. Demanding that the Germans stand up and resist the Nazis, Leaflet No. 4 of the White Rose was searing in its indictment:

> Every word that proceeds from Hitler's mouth is a lie. . . .
> His mouth is the stinking maw of hell and his might is fundamentally reprobate. . . .
>
> . . . Has God not given you the strength, the will to fight? We must attack evil where it is strongest, and it is strongest in the power of Hitler. . . .
>
> We will not keep silent. We are your bad conscience. The White Rose will not leave you in peace!

Arrested for distributing Leaflet No. 6 of the White Rose, the Scholls were brought before Roland Freisler, a notorious Nazi hanging judge. Brother and sister were tried and sentenced to death by beheading, the order to be carried out that very day. Standing before the Nazi court, Sophie was defiant: "Somebody, after all, had to make a start. What we wrote and said is also believed by many others. They just don't dare express themselves as we did." On February 22, 1943, at 5:00 p.m., Hans and Sophie Scholl were executed. Soon after, six other members of the White Rose were arrested and killed. But death would not silence them. Word of the heroic actions of the White Rose reached the Allies. Leaflet No. 6 of the White Rose, the leaflet Sophie and Hans had been caught distributing, was smuggled out of Germany. Soon after, thousands of copies of the leaflets were printed and dropped by Allied planes over the skies above Germany. Even after their deaths, the members of the White Rose continued to haunt the conscience of the German people.

Sophie's cellmate in the Nazi prison kept the indictment on which she had written her final testament for the world, a single German word: *freiheit*.

Freedom.

As the science of awe has revealed, we are most moved to wonder in the face of moral beauty. Our hearts are stirred by the story of the White Rose, the risks the members took and the price they paid to defy Hitler. We are filled with wonder at Sophie Scholl's courage. And the amazement we feel at this story, along with so many others throughout history, brings us back to transcendence.

We are awed by the witness of the White Rose because what they did was true, beautiful, and good, a righteous stand that flowed out of their spiritual and religious convictions. The White Rose embraced, as we've described it, a transcendent narrative identity. They told a sacred story about themselves, about who they were at their moment in history and what they were called to do by way of heroic sacrifice. And the heavy weight of their consciences had what might seem to be a paradoxical effect. The moral demands placed on them by their convictions were not experienced as a burden or bondage, even if it meant being killed. Giving their lives away as an act of sacrificial love was, rather, experienced as freedom and liberation. We gaze in wonder and awe at Sophie Scholl. Standing alone before a Nazi court, there she shines—good, true, and beautiful.

Love is the final step in stepping away from ourselves. Recall that awe creates the experience of a small self, a relational self that is connected to a greater reality, bound up in the larger interests of the world. This small self promotes compassion and love. There is no better example of this than the White Rose. Sophie Scholl told a big story about her life. A story that entangled her fate with the fates of all those who suffered under Hitler. Self-transcendence allowed her to engage in a moral calculus beyond mere self-interest to the point of sacrificing her own life. And we find this heroic act more wondrous than Niagara Falls. More awe-inspiring than the greatest works of art. Love is the most beautiful thing in the world.

Love is the fabric of a meaningful life. Consider research by the psychologists Mengdi Huang and Fan Yang from the University of Chicago. Across a series of studies, Huang and Yang asked people to examine the lives of others through the perspective of either self-transcendence or self-enchantment. For example, various jobs were rated on the degree to which they benefited either *society* (self-transcendence) or the *self* (self-enhancement). Basically, are you working for the good of others or just yourself? Ratings of *happiness* were most correlated with jobs viewed as fulfilling the *self.* By contrast, ratings of the *meaningfulness* of a job were most correlated with *self-transcendence*, where the job was perceived as making a difference in *the lives of others.* Notice how happiness versus meaning hinges on our concerns and what we care about. Meaning in life flows out of *transcendent concerns*, looking *beyond* my own interests to care about the needs of the larger world. Happiness, in contrast, is narrowly concerned with thinking only about yourself.

I don't expect that Sophie Scholl felt happy in the hour before her execution, but there is no doubt, when she wrote the word *freedom* on the back of her indictment, that she found her life deeply and profoundly meaningful. This is another profound paradox, how we find ourselves in giving ourselves away. The late Pope John Paul II called this "the law of the gift." You find yourself to the degree that you give yourself away. You receive your life to the degree that you share it with others as a gift. The Catholic bishop Robert Barron describes the law of the gift this way: "Your being increases in the measure that you give it away. Your being decreases in the measure that you cling to it." As Jesus says in the New Testament, "The one who loses their life will find it." We bear witness to the law of the gift in Sophie Scholl. She gave her life away and called it freedom.

There is something at work in the law of the gift that goes beyond a purely therapeutic approach to achieving joy, something that transcends our concerns regarding self-care, self-help, and self-actualization. Love—true, wonderous, transcendent love—is discovered far beyond the titles of bestselling self-help books. Love isn't a tip, tool, trick, or technique to secure your best life now. Love isn't a life hack. In many ways, love makes life harder, demands things of us, duties we selfishly would rather avoid. This is why love is so awe-inspiring, *that people actually do it.* People love. Every day, and all around us, people transcend their narrow self-interests to care for and sacrifice for others. And if you talk to the Sophie Scholls of the world, they are free and joyous. Having stepped out of the dark caves of self-absorption and self-interest, they have discovered their truest selves in sharing themselves with others. Where we live with the neurotic chatter and exhaustion of our superhero complex, they have discovered the law of the gift.

But despite our wonder, we worry about possible distortions of love. Given how fragile and wounded we all are, isn't a call to give yourself away a recipe for abuse and dysfunction? Won't we lose ourselves if we become wholly other-oriented? What about having healthy boundaries?

By way of reply, let me point out why our conversation in part 2 was so important. Were you to skip those lessons and jump to this final chapter on love, yes, there would be some problems. But everything we talked about in our honeycomb tour of the ego was preparing us for this final step of transcendence. Love is sacrificial. Just ask Sophie Scholl. Or anyone who has ever loved. Consequently, the ego needs to be prepared. Love has to flow out of a secure, self-accepting, and stable identity grounded in a conviction of unconditional mattering. Love comes from ego strength. You cannot give what you do not have. You can't be scared, shamed, manipulated, coerced, or forced into love. Love can only be freely and joyously given. Love is a gift, or it is not love.

And yet, to return to the point, love transcends our concerns about self-care, self-compassion, and self-concern, as vital and necessary as these are in laying the foundation for love. The goal in stabilizing and grounding the ego isn't to remain alone, isolated, and self-protected. The goal is to share our lives with others, to tell that bigger story where my fate becomes entangled with yours. To see this, consider the moral implications of how mindfulness affects our concerns about social repair.

The recovery community describes social repair as "making amends." When we break something, we need to fix it. I remember a conversation I had with my older son, Brenden, after he had a conflict with Jana when he was a teenager. It was a sad situation, as both son and mother were acting in good faith, trying to do the right thing. And yet, through miscommunication and different perceptions, they found themselves on opposite sides of an argument. Reflecting on this sad outcome with Brenden the day after, I shared, "That fight with your mom is one of the tragedies of life. You can do nothing wrong yet still hurt the people you love. There is no escaping it. But we can mend things. That's

THE LAW OF THE GIFT

the labor of love—if we tear something in a relationship, we stay committed to stitching it back together, over and over and over again."

This mending, this constant stitching of a relationship back together again, is social repair. And there are emotions that help us with this, like shame and guilt, that nudge us toward this work. Now, as I expect you know, shame and guilt have fallen on hard times. And people compare and contrast these emotions in all sorts of ways. But no matter how you define them, both shame and guilt are vitally important moral emotions. True, like all emotions, guilt and shame can become excessive and pathological. The way sadness becomes depression or worry becomes an anxiety disorder. But in their natural and healthy bandwidth, both guilt and shame sit at the center of our moral compass, guiding and directing relational behaviors like social repair. If I treat Jana badly, I am haunted by my actions. As I should be. Shame and guilt do their proper and healthy work within my heart, prompting me to make amends, apologize, assume responsibility, and stitch things back together again. We don't ever want to erase shame and guilt from our hearts and minds. We need these emotions. In fact, we have a name for people who lack the capacity for shame and guilt: *sociopath.*

Which brings us back to mindfulness. Mindfulness is a powerful tool in dealing with negative emotions. When we engage with and overidentify with our emotions, they can cascade out of control. We spiral down into depressive rumination or escalate into a panic attack. As we've seen, learning to step away from our emotions with techniques like mindfulness gives us some needed, critical distance from our feelings. And yet some feelings *need to be attended to*, like healthy feelings of guilt and shame nudging us toward social repair. If you've done something wrong and need to apologize, you shouldn't let those feelings go. Appropriate feelings of relational responsibility need to linger to motivate social repair. Negative feelings aren't always bad. And that means mindfulness isn't always healthy and good. Some negative feelings need to pinch and haunt us, and it would be damaging to our relationships to let those feelings go unaddressed. That was the hypothesis guiding research done by the psychologists Andrew Hafenbrack, Matthew LaPalme, and Isabelle Solal.

In their study, Hafenbrack, LaPalme, and Solal examined how mindfulness affected guilt and shame in prompting social repair. What happens when you hurt someone but "let go" of the emotions that are nudging your conscience to say you're sorry and make amends? Generally speaking, using mindfulness to distance yourself from negative emotions is a good thing. But not when you break something in a relationship. While unpleasant, sometimes we need to listen to our conscience. And yet, across five studies they conducted, Hafenbrack, LaPalme, and Solal concluded that mindfulness causes us to avoid our social and moral responsibilities. Mindfulness allowed participants to "let go of" shame and guilt, resulting in them avoiding social repair. Mindfulness thwarted making amends. By letting you off the emotional hook, mindfulness allows you to escape your conscience and avoid your moral duties. Mindfulness lets you get away with hurting people.

The dark side of mindfulness returns us to transcendence and love. Love cannot be reduced to the therapeutic. Love demands more of us than self-care. The obligations we have toward others, especially when we've hurt someone, will intrude and unsettle us. To avoid this discomfort by quickly retreating into self-care is morally irresponsible. There is a voice within us that calls us to the work of social repair and to all the hard duties of love. As we witness in the heroism of the White Rose, beyond entangling our fates, love provides the moral imperative that keeps us entangled when the going gets tough. Love is both compassion *and* conscience, empathy *and* duty. Love is a voice within us that we wish, at times, we could ignore, obligations that we'd rather avoid. But the voice of conscience won't let us go, can even haunt us, until we respond. What we experience in these moments is *friction* between ourselves and a transcendent good. A gap between what love demands and my own selfishness and laziness. The Catholic theologian John Henry Newman described this transcendent aspect of conscience as encountering a voice that "throws us out of ourselves, and beyond ourselves." Sometimes we'd rather stay in the cave, letting mindfulness shoo away pangs of guilt and shame. But love calls us out into the sunlight.

Here with love, we move, fully and finally, beyond ourselves. Our concerns become bound up with the concerns of others. Your life becomes wrapped up in mine, your happiness now linked to my own. And due to this twining, I welcome emotions and obligations into my life that aren't always pleasant. Love worries. Love grieves. Love sacrifices. This is the paradox of the law of the gift. In love, we give to gain. We lose to find. The gift comes back to us.

In the Christian faith tradition, there is a haunting line from the New Testament book of 1 John: "The one who loves knows God." Love and transcendence go hand in hand. Love carries us over the threshold into sacred mystery.

It is true that in our modern world, transcendence can be hard to believe in. We are a very strange people, we who doubt the sun. We harbor suspicions that the true, the beautiful, and the good are figments of our imagination, projecting shapes onto the clouds. I sympathize with the doubt. Maybe it is all an illusion. But the science should haunt the skeptics. Research has shown that the human mind works best when connected with the sacred. The data are in: transcendence is good for you. The sacred grounds your value and allows you to tell a story bigger than the one being told by your superhero complex. Where others see only the ducks of exhaustion, noisy egos, and weariness, we see rabbits of joy, wonder, and gratitude.

But if, here at the end, you still harbor doubts, let me encourage you to consider that ancient advice from 1 John. If you're struggling with the sacred, if transcendence feels vague or imaginary, here's a good first step: Love something. Love another person. Love your garden. Love your pets. Love the earth. Love something true. Love something beautiful. Love something good. For in loving, you'll encounter a reality bigger than yourself. Your ego will grow smaller. You'll be pulled into a relationship with the world. Love will walk you out into the sunlight. Some people who have been tempted by suicide have been able to stave off that dark temptation because no one would be left to water and care for their plants. That thinnest tether of love, sticking around to care for your plants, was enough to keep them connected to life.

If you follow the path of love, some holy, sacred, and invisible facts will come into view. Love is the telescope of transcendence through which you will glimpse a far country. Gaze at the world through love, and you will see.

Not that the journey will be easy. But in the giving, you will receive. A deeply meaningful life awaits you, full of wonder and grace. Love something, and you will discover the law of the gift.

You will trace the shape of joy.

EPILOGUE
The Evangelist of the Plastic Princess Tiara

A pivotal moment of my life, and the origin of this book, happened on the back pew of a small church.

For years, as a college professor and new author, I had been pursuing the vision of success of my particular superhero complex. Your hero game is likely different from mine, but I had become practiced in excelling as a university professor, both inside and outside the classroom. I had won teaching awards, published a pile of journal articles, saw my first book come out, and had gotten tenure. From a professional perspective, I had arrived. And looking down the road, it seemed like the only thing to do was to keep going. Keep my student evaluations high, keep publishing, write another book. More prizes to win, more trophies to collect.

And yet I had come to the point where I found all of this effort—working away at the bike pump of success—wearying. I was tired of the unending project of being myself. My identity felt performative rather than authentic. My accomplishments felt empty and hollow.

Nudged by this restlessness, I became a spiritual seeker. This journey caused me to change social locations. I needed to find

THE SHAPE OF JOY

a different scene. On my campus, I was surrounded by people who were in the grip of my exact superhero complex, everyone exhausted by the bike pumps of teaching, committee work, and research accomplishments. Everyone smoking the cigarettes of professional success, thinking it would be the cure for our status anxieties. Faculty meetings, if you've never attended one, are not very joyful places. Cynicism, stress, burnout, anxiety, exhaustion, insecurity, competition all bubble to the surface. I had to escape.

I started serving out at the prison as a volunteer chaplain. I began to attend a small mission church called Freedom Fellowship. Freedom meets on Wednesday evenings in a poor part of town. We serve a meal for our hungry neighbors with a worship service afterward. I heard stories of beautiful things happening at Freedom, a place where those who were homeless, poor, addicted, mentally ill, cognitively disabled, and formerly incarcerated were being welcomed with love and grace. Freedom was the kind of place I was looking for, somewhere far away from and very different from a college faculty meeting. That's how I found myself one Wednesday evening sitting on the back pew of the church.

The worship at Freedom took some getting used to. I grew up in staid and undemonstrative church communities. The praise services at Freedom were expressive and emotional. Nothing over the top ever happened, no speaking in tongues or people falling to the floor. But there was a lot of hand raising, swaying, and praising the Lord. This uninhibited worship experience embarrassed me at first, but Freedom has been good medicine for me, crippled as I can be by self-consciousness. My ego can become noisy in public spaces due to years of managing my self-presentation in classrooms. I'm no holy roller, but Freedom has loosened me up quite a bit.

The person who captured my heart at Freedom was Miss Beth. Miss Beth had lived a very hard life. She had suffered a lot of abuse, both physical and sexual. She had struggled with addiction, causing her to lose many of her teeth. She had often been homeless. But Miss Beth had found her way to Freedom and had experienced a spiritual transformation. Her life had stabilized, and she became a leader, running the kitchen for the weekly meals. When I showed up at Freedom, Miss Beth was the one who told me where to find the mop.

During our worship services, Miss Beth had a style all her own. Whereas most of us remained in our pews during the praise time, Miss Beth would get up and go to a corner to worship by herself. There she would close her eyes and sway, a gentle rocking motion, as if she were dancing. Which is precisely what she was doing. "Dancing with Jesus" is how Miss Beth described what she was doing during worship. I admit, this sounded strange to me at first. But if you had seen Miss Beth dance, you would have found it beautiful. I've never seen anyone whose spiritual life was infused with such romance. When Miss Beth was dancing with Jesus, she was lovely to behold.

Jana soon joined me at Freedom. For a Valentine's Day party one year, Jana invited the women of Freedom to our home. For many of the women at Freedom, Valentine's Day is a difficult day. Like Miss Beth, many have suffered abuse and rejection. A day created by Hallmark to celebrate romantic love can leave you feeling unwanted, alone, and revisiting a lot of haunting, painful memories. So Jana gathered Miss Beth and the women at Freedom to celebrate a love story they could claim as their own. To add some whimsy in making a very serious point, Jana bought a bunch of plastic princess tiaras from the Dollar Tree, the kind little girls wear pretending to be a Disney princess like Cinderella. At her party, Jana had all the women wear the tiaras to remind themselves that they were, each of them, loved, cherished, and beautiful. And this value—their cosmic, existential mattering—wasn't anything they could either earn or lose. It was simply the truth. A gift. That Valentine's Day, the women placed those plastic princess tiaras on their heads and declared themselves "daughters of the King." In lives where love was painful and scarce, Jesus had loved them. He had made them his own.

What Jana had intended as a beautiful moment for a Valentine's Day party became, for Miss Beth, a calling. That plastic princess tiara fired her imagination. Soon, Miss Beth began to wear a plastic princess tiara at church and pretty much everywhere else. That tiara had become for Miss Beth, whenever she looked into the mirror, a visible reminder of her value and worth. A cheap plastic princess tiara had functioned to bring an invisible fact into view.

Very quickly, Miss Beth grew downright evangelistic about the tiara. Whenever she saw other women struggling with insecurity, shame, or a lack of self-worth, Miss Beth would give them her tiara and share her story. You are loved. You are worthy. All you need to do is receive it as a gift. Wanting to support Miss Beth in her very unique ministry, the church kept her stocked with plastic princess tiaras. Whenever she gave one away, we gave her a replacement. That is how Miss Beth became the evangelist of the plastic princess tiara.

If you came to Freedom, I expect you might have found the sight of Miss Beth a bit odd, even ludicrous. How to make sense of a woman dancing alone with Jesus in a corner, wearing a Dollar Tree princess tiara? Miss Beth probably looked like a crazy person. But as I watched her gentle dance on Wednesday nights, she seemed to me to be the sanest person in the world.

The secret to joy, the mystery of its shape, is that joy doesn't show up as a bullet point on your resume. Joy isn't a summit you climb or a game you win. Joy isn't an accomplishment, a goal you set for yourself like a New Year's resolution. Joy won't be found in your trophy case. Joy is a gift. Joy can't be forced, controlled, or manipulated. You can only receive it with open hands.

The science of transcendence points us beyond ourselves. But it's one thing to read the studies, quite another to live it out. You can know something intellectually but fail to grasp it with your heart. That is where I was, sitting in a pew watching Miss Beth dance. From a purely professional and objective perspective, I showed up at Freedom as a "success." And using that same metric, Miss Beth, by contrast, didn't have much by way of accomplishments. I had more trophies than she did. More bullet points on my resume. And yet a vast psychological and spiritual gulf separated us. I was lost. She was found.

You can read all the studies from the field of positive psychology, but the mystery of joy, happiness, and a meaningful life can be found in Miss Beth's plastic princess tiara. Her identity and worth had been secured in a transcendent source of mattering. And even if you don't share Miss Beth's religious convictions, you can discern the contours of her life, the geometry of her selfhood. You can see the shape of her joy. Miss Beth's mattering came from beyond herself. And because of that, her identity wasn't effort; it was rest.

A few years after that first night when I mopped the floor of her kitchen, Miss Beth was diagnosed with cancer. Jana and I visited her a couple of days before she died.

She was heavily medicated because of the pain. We sat beside her on her hospital bed and softly sang to her, a gospel song she loved. I gently stroked her foot that had come outside of the blankets. With lots of tears, we said goodbye to a woman who had changed my life.

We come, here at the end, gently back to the question I asked my son's graduating class. Who are you on the worst day of your life? On your darkest day, where is your value, your worth, your mattering to be found? Of course, I don't expect you to wear a plastic princess tiara. But I do want you to internalize its sermon, for a sermon it surely is. A sermon backed up with a whole lot of science. On your worst day, your best, and every day in between, your joy will be found in the grace of self-transcendence, in the transformative power of moving beyond yourself.

If you ever visit our little church here in Abilene, Texas, a picture box now hangs in the corner where Miss Beth used to dance her slow dance with Jesus. One of the pictures in the box is of Miss Beth in her kitchen feeding our hungry neighbors. And if you look closely at that picture, you'll see her wearing that Dollar Tree plastic princess tiara.

When I miss my friend, I go and stand in her corner and look at that picture. That corner is, for me, a holy place, a site of sacred pilgrimage. Whenever I begin to lose the thread of my life, when my ego grows loud and the weariness of my superhero complex comes creeping back, I visit that picture of Miss Beth. Staring at her princess tiara, I revisit and recalibrate the geometry of my life. I recall, especially on my worst days, that my worth is a gift.

There are many paths out of the cave and into the sunlight. I pray that you find yours. For my part, I like to look at my friend wearing a tiara.

Shining and beautiful, she reminds me of the shape of joy.

ACKNOWLEDGMENTS

I'd like to express gratitude to the entire Broadleaf Books team for making this book a reality. And a special and heartfelt thank you to Jarrod Harrison for all his encouragement, support, and editorial work.

Thank you to Joel Lawrence, Todd Wilson, Rae Paul, and the Center for Pastoral Theologians for the invitation to share with the CPT psychological perspectives on the virtue of humility. My "hexagon tour" of the ego made its first appearance with those CPT gatherings, and the encouragement and feedback I received from the fellows motivated me to share the hexagon with a larger audience.

As I've shared so many times, thank you to my brothers and sisters at Freedom Fellowship and to the men in the Monday night Bible study at the French Robertson Unit. These two communities have profoundly impacted my life, and for that I am eternally grateful.

Finally, I dedicate this book to Jana. More than any other book I've written, Jana listened as I read chapters aloud at our dining room table, sharing her feedback and encouragement page by page. The messages of this book are woven through our lives in deeply personal and intimate ways. Our story, individually and as a couple, is the story of this book. This is our shared vision about the adventure of love and the shape of joy.

NOTES

INTRODUCTION

Psychological research has shown: T. D. Wilson and D. T. Gilbert, "Affective Forecasting," *Advances in Experimental Social Psychology* 35 (2003): 345–411.

Called "deaths of despair": A. Case and A. Deaton, *Deaths of Despair and the Future of Capitalism* (Princeton, NJ: Princeton University Press, 2020).

"worthy of love and belonging": https://www.ted.com/talks/brene_brown_the_power_of_vulnerability.

I put up the fight of my life: "The Midlife Unraveling," https://brenebrown.com/articles/2018/05/24/the-midlife-unraveling/.

CHAPTER 1

The Centers for Disease Control and Prevention reported that, during the pandemic: "Mental Health, Substance Use, and Suicidal Ideation during the COVID-19 Pandemic," https://www.cdc.gov/mmwr/volumes/69/wr/mm6932a1.htm.

Not surprisingly, we found an easy way: "Alcohol Consumption during the COVID-19 Pandemic: A Cross-Sectional Survey of US Adults," https://www.ncbi.nlm.nih.gov/pmc/articles/PMC7763183/.

COVID-19 didn't kill us, but many of us drank: "Effect of Increased Alcohol Consumption during COVID-19 Pandemic on Alcohol-Associated Liver Disease: A Modeling Study," https://aasldpubs.onlinelibrary.wiley.com/doi/full/10.1002/hep.32272.

As I've said, one of the most consistent findings: G. Lucchetti, H. G. Koenig, and A. L. G. Lucchetti, "Spirituality, Religiousness, and Mental Health: A Review of the Current Scientific Evidence," *World Journal of Clinical Cases* 9, no. 26 (2021): 7620–31.

As Leonard Cohen sings: Leonard Cohen and Rebecca De Mornay, "Anthem," *The Future*, Columbia Records, 1992.

As the old joke goes: The joke here, if you don't know it, concerns how psychoanalysts, in accordance with Freud's psychosexual theory of the mind, had a persistent habit of interpreting every long, cylindrical object (like a cigar) or pointed object (like a spear) within a dream as a phallic symbol. Symbolically, the psychoanalysts insisted, every cigar in your dream was a phallus. Had to be. And the rub was that the analyst couldn't be questioned in their interpretation. Predictably, people started pushing back on the cult-like infallibility of the psychoanalyst and Freud's theory generally. Not every cigar in a dream is a symbolic penis. Sometimes a cigar is just a cigar.

CHAPTER 2

Once upon a time, our problem was guilt: M. B. Crawford, *The World beyond Your Head: On Becoming an Individual in an Age of Distraction* (New York: Farrar, Straus and Giroux, 2015), 165.

In describing this "weariness of the self": A. Ehrenberg, *The Weariness of the Self: Diagnosing the History of Depression in the Contemporary Age* (Montreal: McGill-Queen's University Press), 4.

As Brown describes, "Scarcity is the 'never enough' problem: B. Brown, *Daring Greatly: How the Courage to Be Vulnerable Transforms the Way We Live, Love, Parent, and Lead* (New York: Gotham Books), 26.

For me, and for many of us, our first waking thought: L. Twist, *The Soul of Money: Transforming Your Relationship with Money and Life* (New York: Norton), 43–44.

"is determined by the ratio": James William, *The Principles of Psychology: In Two Volumes* (Newburyport: Dover, 2012).

For example, if you've been successful in achieving "your best life now": Your Best Life Now is the title of a bestselling book written by Joel Osteen.

Here's Leary and Baumeister describing the idea: Mark R. Leary and Roy F. Baumeister, "The Nature and Function of Self-Esteem: Sociometer Theory," *Advances in Experimental Social Psychology* 32 (2000): 1–62.

Author Alain de Botton has described the stress we experience: A. De Botton, *Status Anxiety* (New York: Pantheon Books), vii.

As de Botton describes, our dignity/value: De Botton, *Status Anxiety*, viii.

But the more tragic problem here: Borrowed from the beloved children's book *Alexander and the Terrible, Horrible, No Good, Very Bad Day*.

CHAPTER 3

"heart [was] breaking": https://www.nytimes.com/2016/12/07/us/edgar-welch-comet-pizza-fake-news.html.

Psychologists have observed that conspiracy theories: These three motives are borrowed from Karen Douglas, Robbie Sutton, and Aleksandra Cichocka's "The Psychology of Conspiracy Theories," *Current Directions in Psychological Science* 26 (2017): 538–42.

As Sutton observes, American "apocalypticism": M. A. Sutton, *American Apocalypse: A History of Modern Evangelicalism* (Cambridge, MA: Belknap Press of Harvard University Press), 4.

Whether driven by innately cynical dispositions: Sutton, *American Apocalypse*, 9–10.

Atheist Richard Dawkins describes the world: R. Dawkins, *River out of Eden: A Darwinian View of Life* (New York: Basic Books, 1995), 133.

"to earn a feeling": Becker Ernest, *The Denial of Death* (New York: Free Press, 1973).

Author and essayist Freddie deBoer follows in the footsteps: https://freddiedeboer.substack.com/p/you-arent-the-shit-you-like.

"this can have the effect": Sutton, *American Apocalypse.*

'I lost my income. I wasn't safe': https://newrepublic.com/article
/121861/suey-parkof-cancelcolbert-fame-has-stopped-fighting
-twitter.

Our strongest impulses to discriminate: Sean Westwood et al.,
"The Tie That Divides: Cross-National Evidence of the Pri-
macy of Partyism," *European Journal of Political Research* 57 (2018):
333–54.

The universal prejudice of the superhero complex: W. Storr,
The Status Game: On Social Position and How We Use It (London: William Collins, 2021), 103.

CHAPTER 4

Neuroscientists and psychologists have discovered: M. F.
Mason et al., "Wandering Minds: The Default Network and
Stimulus-Independent Thought," *Science* 315 (2007): 393–95.

As the researchers concluded: M. A. Killingsworth and D. T.
Gilbert, "A Wandering Mind Is an Unhappy Mind," *Science* 330
(2010): 932.

"'going inside' was": E. Kross, *Chatter: The Voice in Our Head, Why It
Matters, and How to Harness It* (New York: Crown, 2021).

Kross describes what science has discovered: *Chatter,* xviii.

Research has found that a quieter ego: H. A. Wayment, J. J. Bauer,
and K. Sylaska, "The Quiet Ego Scale: Measuring the Compassionate Self-Identity," *Journal of Happiness Studies: An Interdisciplinary
Forum on Subjective Well-Being* 16 (2015): 999–1033.

**My doctoral research, for example, was one of the first pub-
lished reviews:** R. Beck and E. Fernandez, "Cognitive-Behavioral Therapy in the Treatment of Anger: A Meta-Analysis,"
Cognitive Therapy and Research 22 (1998): 63–74.

**Multiple studies have also compared CBT with antidepres-
sant medication:** A. C. Butler et al., "The Empirical Status
of Cognitive-Behavioral Therapy: A Review of Meta-Analyses,"
Clinical Psychology Review 26 (2006): 17–21.

For example, research has shown a simple and effective way: E. Kross et al., "Self-Talk as a Regulatory Mechanism: How You Do It Matters," *Journal of Personality and Social Psychology* 106 (2014): 304–24.

Since its introduction, ACT has shown: F. J. Ruiz, "Acceptance and Commitment Therapy versus Traditional Cognitive Behavioral Therapy: A Systematic Review and Meta-Analysis of Current Empirical Evidence," *International Journal of Psychology and Psychological Therapy* 12 (2012): 333–57.

"Contemplation is essentially": Merton Thomas, *Contemplative Prayer* (Garden City, NY: Image Books, 1971).

CHAPTER 5

Humility also protects you from mental health issues: Neal Krause et al., "Humility, Stressful Life Events, and Psychological Well-Being: Findings from the Landmark Spirituality and Health Survey," *Journal of Positive Psychology* 11 (2016): 499–510.

An influential list of these capacities: See June Tangney's article "Humility: Theoretical Perspectives, Empirical Findings and Directions for Future Research," *Journal of Social and Clinical Psychology* 19 (2000): 70–82, and her chapter "Humility," in *Handbook of Positive Psychology*, ed. Snyder and Lopez (New York: Oxford University Press, 2002).

A second influential list, overlapping some: See their article "Humble Beginnings: Current Trends, State Perspectives, and Hallmarks of Humility," *Social and Personality Psychology Compass* 7 (2013): 819–33.

We feel good about ourselves if some "condition of worth": I'm borrowing this term from the famous psychologist Carl Rogers.

CHAPTER 6

The psychologist Dacher Keltner, a world expert: Dacher Keltner, *Awe: The New Science of Everyday Wonder and How It Can Transform Your Life* (New York: Penguin, 2023), 7.

"being amazed": Keltner, *Awe.*

Keltner describes much of what we've already described: Keltner, *Awe*, 33.

In triggering this experience of a smaller: See P. K. Piff et al., "Awe, the Small Self, and Prosocial Behavior," *Journal of Personality and Social Psychology* 108 (2015): 883–99.

CHAPTER 7

I didn't see anything: Beth Moore, *All My Knotted-Up Life: A Memoir* (Carol Stream, IL: Tyndale Momentum, 2023), 112.

Study after study has shown this: See H. G. Koenig, "Religion, Spirituality, and Health: The Research and Clinical Implications," *ISRN Psychiatry* 2012 (2012): 1–33, and D. B. Yaden et al., "A Meta-Analysis of Religion/Spirituality and Life Satisfaction," *Journal of Happiness Studies* 23, no. 8 (2022): 4147.

Consider the insightful 2023 essay: https://www.thenewatlantis .com/publications/therapy-beyond-good-and-evil.

"This relativism, for someone": https://www.thenewatlantis .com/publications/therapy-beyond-good-and-evil.

"exhausted from carrying": https://www.thenewatlantis.com /publications/therapy-beyond-good-and-evil.

"to search for values": https://www.thenewatlantis.com/publica tions/therapy-beyond-good-and-evil.

"sense of reality": James William, *The Varieties of Religious Experience* (Mineola, NY: Dover, 2002).

As Dacher Keltner describes, in summarizing: Keltner, *Awe*, 11.

CHAPTER 8

So I stuck to the science: See G. L. Flett, *The Psychology of Mattering: Understanding the Human Need to Be Significant* (London: Elsevier Academic Press, 2018).

But at the end of the day, the research has shown: See Michael Prinzing, Patty Van Cappellen, and Barbara L. Fredrickson, "More than a Momentary Blip in the Universe? Investigating the Link between Religiousness and Perceived Meaning in Life," *Personality and Social Psychology Bulletin* 49 (2023): 180–96.

This might surprise you, but loneliness: "Our Epidemic of Loneliness and Isolation: The US Surgeon General's Advisory on the Healing Effects of Social Connection and Community" (Washington, DC: Office of the US Surgeon General, 2023).

"Participants who reported": "Our Epidemic of Loneliness and Isolation."

"positive regard": C. R. Rogers, "A Theory of Therapy, Personality, and Interpersonal Relationships: As Developed in the Client-Centered Framework," In *Psychology: A Study of a Science. Formulations of the Person and the Social Context,* ed. S. Koch (New York: McGraw Hill, 1959), 3:184–256.

Beyond, behind, beneath all solid things: F. Spufford, *Unapologetic: Why, despite Everything, Christianity Can Still Make Surprising Emotional Sense* (New York: HarperOne, 2023), 57–65.

CHAPTER 9

Psychologists have described these experiences: See Patty Van Cappellen, "Rethinking Self-Transcendent Positive Emotions and Religion: Insights from Psychological and Biblical Research," *Psychology of Religion and Spirituality* 9, no. 3 (2017): 254–63.

In his influential work on emotions: Robert C. Roberts, "Joy and the Nature of Emotion," *Journal of Positive Psychology* 15, no. 1 (2020): 30–32.

According to psychological research, meaning in life: Laura A. King and Joshua A. Hicks, "The Science of Meaning in Life," *Annual Review of Psychology* 72 (2021): 61–84.

Of these three ingredients, as we've discussed: Vlad Costin and Vivian L. Vignoles, "Meaning Is about Mattering: Evaluating Coherence, Purpose, and Existential Mattering as Precursors of Meaning in Life Judgments," *Journal of Personality and Social Psychology: Personality Processes and Individual Differences* 118 (2020): 864–84.

In describing these stories, psychologist Pamela King: See Pamela Ebstyne King, "Joy Distinguished: Teleological Perspectives on Joy as a Virtue," *Journal of Positive Psychology* 15 (2020): 33–39.

Research has shown that gratitude and joy: Philip C. Watkins et al., "Joy Is a Distinct Positive Emotion: Assessment of Joy and Relationship to Gratitude and Well-being," *Journal of Positive Psychology* 13 (2018): 522–39.

The psychological power of gratitude: Florencio F. Portocarrero, Katerina Gonzalez, and Michael Ekema-Agbaw, "A Meta-Analytic Review of the Relationship between Dispositional Gratitude and Well-being," *Personality and Individual Differences* 164 (2020): 110101.

CHAPTER 10

Every word that proceeds from: "The White Rose Leaflets," Revolt and Resistance, Holocaust Research Project, December 10, 2015.

Consider research by the psychologists: Mengdi Huang and Fan Yang, "Self-Transcendence or Self-Enhancement: People's Perceptions of Meaning and Happiness in Relation to the Self," *Journal of Experimental Psychology: General* 152, no. 2 (2023): 590–610.

"the law of the gift": John Paul, *Love and Responsibility* (Boston: Pauline Books & Media, 2013).

"Your being increases": https://wordonfire.podbean.com/e/the-law-of-the-gift/.

And people compare and contrast these emotions: Brené Brown has popularized defining shame as focused on the *self* and guilt on *behavior*. Shame is "I am bad," and guilt is "I did something bad."

That was the hypothesis guiding research: A. C. Hafenbrack, M. L. LaPalme, and I. Solal, "Mindfulness Meditation Reduces Guilt and Prosocial Reparation," *Journal of Personality and Social Psychology* 123, no. 1 (2022): 28–54.

"throws us out of ourselves": Newman John Henry, *Sermons Preached on Various Occasions* (Westminster, MD: Christian Classics, 1968).